Business Process Reengineering

An Executive Resource for Implementation

Business Process Reengineering
An Executive Resource for Implementation

by

Harold S. Resnick

Contributing Principals:

Terence W. Garland

Donald J. Grasso

Richard M. Jones

Norbert J. Salz

Paul F. Stimson

Work Systems Associates, Inc.
313 Boston Post Road West
Marlborough, MA 01752
508.460.0404

Business Process Reengineering: An Executive Resource for Implementation

ISBN 0-9644468-4-7

Printed in the United States of America

For further information regarding the availability of this book, contact:

Work Systems Associates, Inc.
313 Boston Post Road West
Marlborough, MA 01752
508.460.0404

Table of Contents

	Acknowledgements	vii - viii
	Preface	ix - xi
	Executive Summary	xiii - xviii
Chapter One	The Call for Change	Pages 1-30
Chapter Two	The Role of Leadership	Pages 31-60
Chapter Three	The Role of Teams in Business Process Reengineering	Pages 61-94
Chapter Four	The Reengineering Process and Tools	Pages 95-130
Chapter Five	Measuring Results	Pages 131-146
	Bibliography	Pages 147-152

Acknowledgements

No book can be written and produced without the concerted effort of a team of people working together. This is even more true if the book is based on the business practice of a consulting firm, and the work of that firm as implemented by the consultants and the support team.

This book is the natural extension of the work of the firm. Work Systems Associates, Inc. has done far more than serve as the publisher for this book. It has been the source of the inspiration, the work, and the physical and moral support that has made it possible.

The author is indebted to the clients of the firm. We have been privileged to work with them, learn and grow with them, and collaborate in solving problems and increasing the effectiveness of our respective organizations. Particular appreciation is extended to CH2M HILL, Inc.; to Volvo GM Heavy Truck Corporation; to Barclays' Bank - Business Credit; and to the Pioneer Grain Division of James Richardson & Sons, Ltd. These companies have been partners with Work Systems in every spirit of the word, and have contributed much to the intellectual growth that made this book possible.

Much of the seminal work in reengineering grew from our work in continuous improvement/total quality. The Raytheon Company partnered with us in this area for many years and we would like to acknowledge their contribution to our growth and thinking.

Everyone at Work Systems made a distinct contribution to the development of this book. All the consultants were actively engaged in the process.

Some authored sections; others contributed as editors or critical reviewers.

Special thanks go to Terry Garland who developed many of the models that are represented in this text.

The members of the Work Systems support team also contributed in very special ways. Amy Meehan provided the glue that held the book together in its developmental stages through the first round of completed copy. Sandi Alicandro, Lisa Schofield and Debby Booth served as the graphics team that designed and prepared the book in its current form. Robin Davis, Barbara Lane, and Chris McLeod provided critical reviews and editorial support through many versions in the final weeks before production. Sue Mandel coordinated the final processes that brought this project to completion.

This book is not the work of a single person, or a single team. It represents the evolution of our thinking as it has matured and been practiced with clients.

Harold S. Resnick
November, 1994

Preface

To initiate a reengineering effort requires both courage and encouragement, so allow me to start by sharing some promising results. Our engagement of process reengineering, with the aid of Work Systems Associates, has spawned very significant breakthroughs, far exceeding our expectations. The results, thus far, have included permanent and positive organizational changes coupled with an expanding confidence in our company's ability to embrace the changing world successfully. The results of reengineering to date have both enhanced our customer focus by improving capabilities to better meet their current demands, and created breakthrough thinking that is expanding our services to meet our customer's future needs. We are now able to capture more of the collective mental horsepower of our company as empowerment and confidence in the process matures. The recipe for the success we have experienced in our journey of change is what this book is about.

Key ingredients for the recipe begin with the "Why?" part of change. The fundamentals of global competitiveness and our changing world are well addressed by the author. The challenge and the work of "Why" is the acceptance and understanding that change is needed. Fortunately, our customers were impatient and demanded radical redesign. They simply would not wait for incremental improvements through TQM, although they also valued the significant improvement we were starting to make through our Quality Initiative. The challenge was to convince our "benchmark" thinking company that we had areas where improvement was mandatory and urgent. This required the second key ingredient of leadership.

Peter Drucker says it well: "Leadership is Vision!!" The author of this book agrees and defines transformational leadership (the leadership of change) as the kind that produces vision, generates alignment to that vision, and defines the parameters of deployment. This is very different from the command and control management we have become so accustomed to in our organizational life. The leadership ingredient for reengineering cannot be successful unless it starts from the top. We were fortunate to have this asset at the beginning of reengineering.

Once leadership is in place, empowered work teams, following the recipe (the process), perform the work of process reengineering. The author has provided valuable details regarding team construction, direction and chartering (the licence to act) as well as defining the expected behaviors for success. Based on my experience, this guidance is very clearly directed since well intended people very often find it difficult to apply team work behaviorally even while intellectually acknowledging its recognized benefits. Some people tend to be very impatient, highly individualistic and have most of "the answers" well before work begins. Teamwork, following a prescribed process for reengineering, is truly a learning experience and outside coaches can add significant value and ensure high performance.

The process of reengineering (the recipe) is the meeting place for all ingredients. If followed, it becomes the producer of very positive outcomes. Once again, the author has carefully outlined an experienced-based process and suggests a variety of tools that may be used.

Unquestionably, the work is here and the benefits of reengineering depend to large degree on how well the process is followed. This process is not for the fainthearted. It requires a willingness to undergo critical self-analysis, to encounter change of the broadest and deepest kind, and to maintain the discipline required of a rigorous process. Finally, implementation of the reengineered processes, including the performance measurements, is the capstone of the effort and requires work that should not be underestimated.

The challenge to all of us is to have the Courage To Act.

S. David Ellison, P.E.
Senior Vice President, Quality Improvement
CH2M HILL, Inc.

Executive Summary

We live in a time of transformation. Not since the Industrial Revolution that fundamentally changed the economic and socio-political shape of the world have we seen times as turbulent as these. The very fabric of the economic structure of society is being ripped apart and reshaped in one vast movement. And, because of the technological advances of this past century, the pace of this change is occurring so rapidly that entire industries are being formed - or destroyed - in a mere decade.

Joel Barker, a futurist who has contributed to our understanding of the implications of major "paradigm" shifts, describes one of the fundamental principles as: "When the rules change, everyone goes back to zero." This leads to two questions: What are the rules that are changing and how do I push the "reset" button if we are all back at zero?

This book endeavors to describe the core principles or rules that characterize this shift, as well as the methodologies, tools and techniques that can be used to guide an organization through this sea of change. A few of the core shifting principles are as follows.

1. Our organizations are shifting from a fragmented, functional orientation in thinking about their business to a process-driven integrated approach to examining how the work actually gets done. This confronts all traditional rules regarding organization hierarchy and power bases. It demands a shift from a task to a process orientation model for management.

2. Individual performance based on stable, defined responsibilities shifts to a team performance model with responsibilities for greater flexibility to meet the requirements of the organization.

3. Management structures, systems and behavioral models, therefore, must also shift from a "command and control" hierarchical approach to a participative, "coaching and counseling" model for guiding and supporting the behavior and performance of others.

4. The psychological work contract shifts from loyalty and obedience in exchange for long-term security to performance-based results in exchange for long term employability and opportunity. Compensation shifts from security and predictability to risk-based models derived from individual, team and organization performance.

5. The increasing sophistication of customers, along with rapidly expanding skilled competitive forces, have simultaneously "raised the performance bar" not just for today's products and services but in the realization that standing still amounts to being overtaken in the briefest of moments.

6. The force of the organization shifts from an internally driven, growth and profit-centered focus to an external customer satisfaction focus, with profitability as the outcome rather than the driver of successful organization performance.

7. Advances in technology have fundamentally altered established management models. With computers that instantly provide access to information and knowledge at all levels of the organization, some of the traditional roles for "middle management" to gather, disseminate and control information are no longer needed. The implication of data converted to information, to knowledge and then to wisdom is just beginning to be realized.

The business community has attempted to respond to these, and other major changes in a variety of ways. Some have reacted by "waiting the storm out" and hoping for a period returning to normalcy. This is the shortest path to extinction. Unfortunately, there are a significant number of organizations that will choose extinction over change, just as many individuals choose death over long-term preventive personal health care such as exercise and diet.

Other organizations have chosen a "slow but steady" evolutionary approach to change. This may be successful in relatively stable and highly capital intensive environments. The caution that must be exerted, however, is the "boiled frog" syndrome. Slow and steady change is often overtaken by fundamentally different approaches that are not even noticed while they occur.

Total quality management is a major change initiative that recognizes the need for overall transformational change and uses teams to drive this change through process improvement. For many organizations, it has had a profound impact on the organization's culture and performance levels. Unfortunately, it has had a significantly lesser impact on many others. Although the reasons vary, the lack of sustained permanent change is often attributable to lack of sustained senior leadership.

Many organizations have selected more of a "shock wave" approach to massive change. The shock wave requires mandated senior level leadership; breaks down existing structures and systems; is often driven by technological requirements or opportunities; and has the potential for improvements measured by orders of magnitude rather than incremental gains.

This is the opportunity - and challenge - of reengineering. Reengineering asks the fundamental business questions regarding vision, direction, strategy, marketplace positioning and customer requirements. Then it reshapes the organization from a clean piece of paper. Reengineering means that the old is not repaired but rather replaced with a completely new model or approach.

Reengineering occurs on two levels: for the entire organization and for core business processes. Organizational level reengineering addresses the organization's vision and strategy; its basic organizational structure; all its systems and processes; human resource and cultural concerns; and the tools and technology required to support the reengineered organization.

Business process reengineering offers the opportunity to examine and redesign major business processes without necessarily restructuring the entire organization. It is important to recognize, however, that it is still a major organizational undertaking that should not be taken lightly. It is not for the faint of heart. Reengineering has significant cultural implications regarding management styles, teamwork, cross-functional collaboration, reduction of bureaucracy and hierarchy, free flow of information and knowledge, and increased customer focus.

Also it often has technological, capital equipment and system implications that require serious thought and investment.

Our experience has continuously validated the premise that, in the end, it all comes down to people. If people have consistent and common clarity of vision and purpose; are empowered to truly change the organization; are provided with the skills and methodologies required to successfully perform the work; and are given the resources and technology needed to support their efforts, they can achieve remarkable results.

Reengineering in itself is not such a challenging technological barrier that it can only be implemented by the elite few. Stated in the vernacular: "It's not rocket science." The real barrier to reengineering is the continual support and commitment of senior leadership, along with the systems required to sustain the effort.

This book describes the reason, the process, the methodology, the tools, the measurements, and the support required for the success of business process reengineering. We have found through our experience with many firms in the manufacturing and service industries, both public and private, large and small alike, that the methods described here work. We have applied them both with our clients and internally within our own firm, with similar success. We invite you to do the same and to enjoy both the journey and the results.

H. S. R.

Chapter One

The Call for Change

World Events: The Shifting Economic Model

The Challenge: New Realities

We live in the last days of the industrial model that has dominated world economics throughout the twentieth century. It is a time of profound and rapid change, the size and scope of which are symbolized by the fact that we are coming to the end of a century. Centuries not only define historical time, they represent and bring to mind overriding themes, beliefs, and ways of organizing our political, social and economic lives. If we are going to successfully deal with these transformational times, we must be clear about where we are coming from, as well as understanding where we are going.

Organizations and leaders find themselves in the middle of complex change forces coming from a variety of internal and external sources. They must be able to cope with changing conditions in ways that improve individual and team performance, as well as organizational functioning.

What are some of the key changes in today's business world?

- Technological shifts in information availability and processing power virtually eliminate information float
- The world is more competitive and competitors come from outside our traditional core businesses
- Margins are thinner, with severe impact on cost structures
- Customers are less loyal, but more sophisticated and more demanding
- We are all competing in a global economy; geographic boundaries have become almost incidental
- Product and technological competitive advantages are short-lived at best

World Events: The Shifting Economic Model

Megatrends of Change

Many social observers have noted and described the important changes taking place in the United States and the rest of the world. John Naisbet used the term "megatrends" to give a sense of how dynamic and radical these changes can be.

Typically we see megatrends in three basic areas: Economic, Technical, and Social / Cultural. We have seen numerous traditional changes in each of these three areas and are current witnesses to many more emerging trends. The chart below defines some of these changes to give us a better understanding of what is happening in our shifting society and the world around us.

Area	Traditional	The New Model
Economic	• Industrial age • Assembly-line production • Stable markets and suppliers • Domestic competition	• Information age • Customization of products and services • Fluid markets and suppliers • International competition
Technical	• Mechanical technology • Predictable technological innovation (10 years)	• Electronic technology • Rapid, unpredictable technological innovation (18 months)
Social / Cultural	• Authoritarian hierarchical work, roles and structures • Task and activity focus • Stable homogeneous work force • Work primarily based on individual responsibility	• Horizontal organizational structures and more employee involvement • Process and results focus • Diversity in the workplace • Work as a team responsibility

World Events: The Shifting Economic Model

Challenges of Organizational Transformation

Change is a recognized requirement among leading organizations today. The world around us - the economy, marketplace, competitors, customers, and our own internal forces demands responses that are different from the past. The challenge, however, is that both the scope and pace of change are occurring at an unprecedented rate. We live in a world where success is defined by those able to ride the waves of constant change. Steering the ship of our organizations has shifted from dealing with periods of turbulence amid relatively calm seas to continuous, relentless white water rafting.

Change in itself is not new. However, the extent of the change required by organizations to respond to the challenges of today's business environment is broad and far-reaching. Change of this scope impacts the organization's:

- Vision, mission, goals, and core values
- Management structures and organizational models
- Work systems and processes
- Performance expectations and behaviors at individual and team levels
- Reward and recognition systems with increased emphasis on empowerment and mutual risk

The New Business Model

**Key Factors
That Define
Success in
the 90's**

In short, the new "world order" reflects a requirement for comprehensive change for those organizations seeking to transform themselves into top performing leaders in the globally competitive marketplace.

In this constantly changing world, there are four key factors that must remain consistently effective to ensure an organization's success:

1. Quality of products and services.

2. Customer Satisfaction met by identifying needs and requirements, and meeting them at all points in the process of delivering the product or service.

3. Performance of Operational Systems and Processes through continuous improvement by all individuals.

4. Use of Teams to Improve Performance and Productivity. Top performing organizations have learned that implementing teams to manage and improve key processes of the business is an essential way to generate improved performance and an empowered organization.

The New Business Model

The Globally Competitive Organization

The following characteristics are common to globally competitive organizations:

- Marketplace driven - global perspective
- Clarity of vision, focus and direction
- Customer driven
- Innovative and responsive to shifting needs
- Goal oriented with measurable outputs
- Process centered
- Team oriented with focus on continuous improvement
- Structured to minimize hierarchy and empower the workforce
- Self critical and able to learn from experience
- Profitable

The Shifting Culture

The shifts from the industrial model of the past to the emerging business model demanded by the new economy can be categorized as follows:

1. External Focus and Direction

2. Organizational Culture and Practices

3. Individual and Team Work

The New Business Model

The Shifting Culture

The statements below outline the key shifts that help an organization become more successful in today's global business environment.

External Focus and Direction

- The global marketplace - best in class wherever it exists in the world is the new performance benchmark for all competitors
- Sustained competitive advantage is driven by quality and service, not product and technology
- Customized products replacing volume-driven production
- Long term success based on sustained customer satisfaction, not quarterly profits alone

Organizational Culture and Practices

- Leadership is focused on vision, alignment and deployment
- Management is focused on continuous process improvement
- Standards of quality are set by the marketplace and customer
- Organizational structure is designed to maximize customer satisfaction and responsiveness; not command and control

Individual and Team Work

- Individual work includes process improvement and personal development
- Focus shifts from pleasing the boss to satisfying customers
- The work contract shifts from individual loyalty rewarded by job security to empowerment and rewards based on performance and innovation
- Performance is based on team performance as well as individual work

The New Business Model

**The New
Integrated
Business
Model**

The following diagram shows the integrated business model developed by Work Systems that describes how an organization should guide its work with both customer focus and process improvement woven throughout the fabric of the business.

Vision

Vision is increasingly recognized as one of the most significant differentiators characterizing global leaders across industries. Vision setting includes the established internal and external environmental scans and analyses traditionally associated with strategic planning. That, however, is simply the validation of the basis for a vision. Vision captures the emotional spirit by defining a dream that embodies the soul and spirit of the organization. The president of a manufacturing company we are working with said that "vision supplies the generative life blood to the organization. Our vision not only keeps us alive it fosters our growth and development." From this vision, values and guiding principles can be crafted that provide direction and broad boundaries, yet enable individuals to act with independence, judgement, and initiative - the essence of empowerment. Setting vision may well be the single most important responsibility of leadership.

Alignment

Alignment is the process by which the organization is able to convert its vision, values, and guiding principles into a defined high level plan. That is, core internal and external strategies must be derived that will enable the vision to become a reality. From these broad strategies specific goals and measures are then crafted that guide the work of the organization. Goals embrace the established "steady state" performance requirements as well

The New Business Model

as continuous improvement, new initiatives and customer and workforce focus. The process of creating both understanding and then commitment to these strategies and goals at all points across the organization is the next primary responsibility of leadership. Through alignment, all of the organization's energy and actions are consolidated, focused, and pointed in an agreed upon direction.

Deployment

Peter Drucker has often been accused of authoring the comment: "Everything degenerates into work." Regardless of authorship, real work is the act of applying resources as needed to achieve the agreed upon goals of the organization. Defining where and how to deploy these resources is the act of leadership. Executing this deployment is the day-to-day work of the organization, the guidance of which defines the management function. The model shown indicates that work is performed at the individual, functional team, and cross-functional team level. The measures of success include the traditional measures defined by functional areas. Among leading organizations, they also embrace concepts of customer satisfaction, continuous improvement of work processes, and performance management applied to both individual and team work performance.

Traditional organizations tend to be consumed by their day-to-day steady state activities. They require all their resources to deliver their products and services to the marketplace. Managers have the primary role of defining the work, telling others what to do to execute this work, and then monitoring work performance to ensure its satisfactory completion. This is the embodiment of the classic "command and control" management model.

The New Business Model

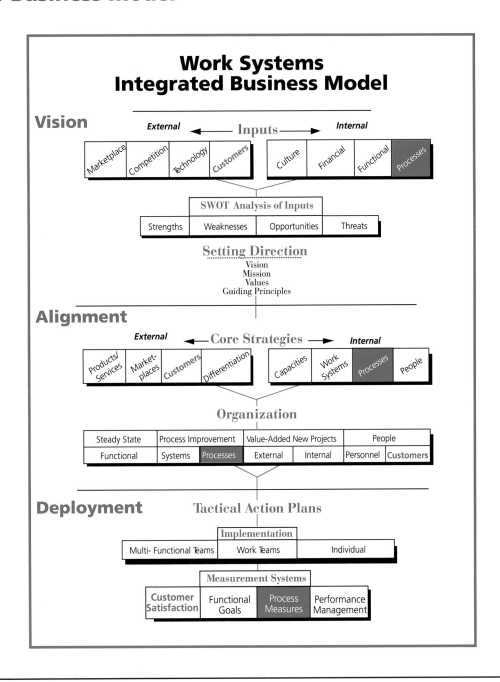

The New Business Model

The New Integrated Business Model

The model presented here is designed to highlight several key distinctions of how a business should govern itself in the evolving business world. First, the distinction between management and leadership is defined and articulated in behavioral terms: what managers and leaders do, rather than simply distinctions in personal or interpersonal style. Leaders create vision, generate alignment to that vision, and define the parameters of deployment. Managers execute deployment to ensure that the goals and objectives of the organization are achieved.

Secondly, this model shows how customer focus is woven throughout all phases of the organization's work. Customer focus is not achieved through a special program or a periodic survey. Rather, it is part of the fabric of the vision and goals, integrated into all operational processes and activities, and one of the key measurements of success. Similarly, process deployment and process improvement run through the fabric of the organization. Processes cannot be addressed only through TQM or reengineering programs. They are the vehicle by which work is performed. Defining and guiding these processes is the ongoing responsibility of both leaders and managers. This business model shows how the strategic planning process, the goal setting process, and all organizational activities should be treated as an integrated whole to achieve the goals of the organization and create delighted customers.

Determining Your Core Business Processes

Strategies   Reengineering is the complete redesign of a process to bring it into alignment with its vision, purpose, and critical success factors. Organizational processes should be identified and then examined using a structured approach to determine where reengineering will create the greatest benefit. This section provides strategies to identify core business processes, and then determines how to break them down into smaller components which may be more suitable for reengineering.

Most companies have defined their core business processes. This step is key to beginning a reengineering effort since it helps focus management on the important areas where work gets done. Some organizations find it difficult to determine their core business processes because they tend to think in terms of departments or functions, not in terms of the work they actually do, and the manner in which this work is performed. Cross-functional processes often go unmanaged because rarely is there an identified process owner - one person responsible for ensuring that the process is well defined; capable of achieving its intended results; and executed with fidelity to ensure that all the steps in the process are carried out as designed.

How can organizations identify their core business processes if they have not already done so? One useful technique is to name processes in such a way that they identify their beginning and their end. For example, the sales generation process could be called the "Prospect to Order Process." If we simply said "the sales process" we might list all the tasks and activities conducted by the sales department. "Prospect to Order" may well include

Determining Your Core Business Processes

steps that are not structurally housed in the sales department. Naming the processes in this way helps break the structured, usually functional paradigm, and focuses on the work people do.

A critical step that many organizations miss is recognizing the affinity between these core businesses processes and their "core competencies." Core business processes should always consider the core competencies of an organization.

A company can have several hundred processes but most companies have between five and ten core business processes. The chart on the following page details core business processes for three leading companies.

The examples shown on the opposite page from IBM, Xerox, and British Telecom represent the breadth and cross-functional nature of core business processes. Without one of these core processes, it could be said that an organization would, in effect, cease to function. This can be a useful yardstick in measuring whether or not a core process has been identified. Some organizations choose to map the processes in an organization. Mapping makes it easy to break them down further. Tree diagramming is a very useful tool for this exercise. The initial processes identified should be the core processes only. Once these are determined and mapped, it becomes easy to break them down further using the tree diagram model.

Determining Your Core Business Processes

IBM	Xerox	British Telecom
Market information capture	Customer engagement	Direct business
Market selection requirements	Inventory management and logistics	Plan business
Development of hardware	Product design and engineering	Develop processes
Development of software	Product maintenance	Manage process operation
Development of services	Technology management	Provide personnel support
Production	Production and operations management	Market products and services
Customer fulfillment	Market management	Provide customer service
Customer relationship	Supplier management	Manage products and services
Service	Information management	Provide consultancy services
Customer feedback	Business management	Plan the network
Marketing	Human resource management	Operate the network
Solution integration	Leased and capital asset management	Provide support services
Financial analysis	Legal	Manage information resources
Plan integration	Financial management	Manage finance
Accounting		Provide technical R&D
Human resources		
IT infrastructure		

*Davenport, Thomas H. **Process Innovation: Reengineering Work Through Information Technology.** Boston: Harvard Business School Press, 1993. Pp. 29.*

Determining Your Core Business Processes

Strategies   Processes are developed from left to right on a tree diagram. The question is asked: What processes must be performed at the next level to achieve the larger process? When completed, the analysis is subjected to the "necessary and sufficient" test. From left to right, the question is asked: If these processes are all performed, are they sufficient to achieve the process on the left? From right to left, the question is asked: Are all these processes necessary to achieve the larger process on the left?

The first level of processes in a tree diagram typically yields five to ten core processes that define the business. At the second level, approximately 30 processes are typically identified. These are still at a relatively high level and have clear owners, usually senior managers and executives. The third level tends to generate approximately 100 processes. These are often the most troublesome for the organization. They are still large enough to be cross-functional. However, they often do not have any clear process owners. The fourth level generates 400-500 processes which are typically resident within functional departments. These define the individual and small, intact team work and are also typically well known and understood.

The following process map is a high-level representation of the core processes for a leading large truck manufacturer. Although not a typical tree diagram, this map shows the core processes. The key items to notice are that it identifies only its five core business processes and the strategic drivers that set the performance criteria for their processes.

Determining Your Core Business Processes

Once these core processes have been identified, each one should be exploded into the subprocesses that comprise it. This helps focus the reengineering efforts even further, to look at which aspects of a core business process may not be working the way we want them to. Process mapping can be difficult because it requires everyone to think organizationally, not departmentally. But in its finished form, it should be clear and obvious that "that is what we do."

Another way to break these core processes down further is to do a macro overview of the major supplier-process-customer relationships in the organization. Within each of these core processes, for example, there may be 6 to 36 others, each with a defined supplier, process, and customer. Once all these relationships are defined within a core process, they are sufficiently broken down into performance elements to be analyzed for possible reengineering.

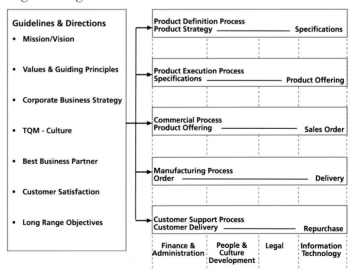

When and Whether to Reengineer

Organizational Signals   Reengineering is a serious undertaking. It forces a fundamental examination of the core purpose of the key processes to be reengineered, and may require a major adjustment of many of the ways in which the organization conducts its business.   Therefore, now that we have identified the core business processes, we must look for signals or symptoms that the reengineering of any one or more of these processes is necessary.   Some of these signals might be:

1.   The process is so poor that it creates competitive disadvantage.

2.   The process is so dysfunctional that it is virtually ignored by the organization and replaced with "work arounds."

3.   The process is so inefficient that urgent needs (which happen regularly) are "walked through" the process to meet requirements.

4.   Customers express dissatisfaction based on the lack of performance of the process.

5.   Bureaucracy prevails and there does not seem to be a way to increase the efficiency or effectiveness of the process.

6.   Political issues dominate segments of the process and are treated as "that's the way it is and there's nothing we can do about it."

When and Whether to Reengineer

7. New products or services require a different result and the current process cannot meet these new requirements.

8. Changes in the organization's vision or goals require a different method that cause the current process to be obsolete.

9. Technological advances and tools require that the process be redesigned to enable the new technology to fulfill its potential.

Criteria for Determining When to Reengineer

The next step is to analyze these signals in the light of reengineering. In order to do this we must have a clear and factual analysis of what is happening in the marketplace. We must identify our core capabilities and compare them to what our competition is doing. We must also identify our company vision and see how well our core business processes and capabilities align with this vision. By conducting this analysis, we begin to understand how to turn these external and internal signals to our advantage.

There are generally three positions from which organizations can consider reengineering.

Reengineering from a position of strength. Organizations can consider enhancing a competitive advantage and thus widening the gap between themselves and the competition.

Reengineering from a position of anticipating problems. Organizations can project, based on marketplace analysis, what they will and will not

When and Whether to Reengineer

Criteria for Determining When to Reengineer

need to do in the future and can reengineer early before these situations arise.

Reengineering from a position of weakness. An organization's survival may be in the balance if it does not conduct a radical "jumpstart" in the way it conducts and delivers its core business. Of course, not all processes can be reengineered simultaneously. How then can an organization determine which process should be given the highest priority? There are three criteria on which to base this decision.

Dysfunction: Which processes are providing the poorest performance?
Importance: Which processes have the greatest impact on customers?
Feasibility: Which processes are most likely to be successful in redesign?

Criteria for Determining Whether to Reengineer

Not all processes necessarily need reengineering. Some may simply need incremental improvements or stabilization. When looking at a process that seems not to be working, you must determine whether it is truly a reengineering effort that this process requires. If incremental improvements are needed, a process improvement team can very likely create the desired result. If the process needs to be stabilized, a new measurement system and control tools may provide the solution. Reengineering should only be attempted if the process requires a major performance improvement and it appears that modification will not be sufficient. It is also not unusual to find, as one of our engineering clients recently discovered, that once high level organizational reengineering is completed, exciting opportunities for process improvements at all levels begin to emerge. A culture and climate for continuous improvement often develops.

When and Whether to Reengineer

The most difficult decision to make is not when to reengineer but whether to reengineer. Reengineering is not always the answer to an organization's troubles. A comprehensive external and internal analysis must first be done to determine factors that are influencing the organization's performance. The core processes and capabilities should be benchmarked against the competition to determine why they are failing and if they are actually failing. If one area of the business is incapable of meeting customer needs in such areas as product customization, order fulfillment or speed, then the organization must make a decision whether to reengineer. It may have other alternatives that would enhance the organization's competitive position. The key is to know precisely where the competition provides a threat and then apply a strategy for success.

Scoping the Reengineering Project

The decision to go ahead with the reengineering of a core business process forces the executive team to determine the scope that the initiative is going to take. This at first may seem a relatively simple undertaking.

However, further exploration of the complexity of core business processes and their inherent cross-functional and interdependent nature can often obscure the necessity of including critical pre and post elements of the process as well as the critical interfaces with other core business processes. Not adequately understanding these issues can tend to initially restrict the parameters of the process and thus diminish the success of the initiative to meet the reengineering goals and the vision for the process.

When and Whether to Reengineer

Scoping the Reengineering Project

Scoping the reengineering project requires determinations in five areas:

1. Have a clear definition of the beginning and end of the process.

2. Determine what you want to achieve out of the process and relate that to the boundary conditions you set.

3. Determine the time over which reengineering will occur and when the expectation of results will be achieved.

4. Identify the perceived amount of resources to be utilized in the effort.

5. Understand the interface implications and changes.

An effective scoping must incorporate a clear knowledge of what is to be achieved by the reengineering within the boundaries of the project. Initially prescribing too rigid a set of parameters on the process to be reengineered was exemplified by a recent client, a major commercial world bank, who engaged our services in reengineering their order fulfillment process. The President initially set the process vision and defined the beginning and end points of the process. The process went from the point at which an intent to approve the loan was made through the confirmation of the delivery of the loan. Part of this included due diligence to verify the client's credit worthiness. This initial scope ignored two vital aspects of their order fulfillment process: the activities that led to the decision of a letter of intent; and the impact on clients due to the extensive lag time between the loan

When and Whether to Reengineer

confirmation and the actual funds reaching the client's account. The timelag proved to have a long term negative effect on the client's decision to renew the loan commitment, and for new clients to engage the bank.

The problem, on further examination, was systemic. The established process reinforced the behaviors of the business development officers to hand hold the deal through the underwriting process. Initial boundary conditions excluded this from the process. Analysis of the process during a strategic session with the steering team brought this to light and allowed the scope to be broadened and redefined.

Scoping a reengineering initiative requires an understanding of the time span needed and an expectation of when the reengineered process will be complete, with results positively impacting the organization. An assessment of the resources to be utilized in the effort needs to take place. The actions that need to be taken at key interface points, which may further change the scope originally envisioned, must also be considered.

Consequences to the Organization

Benefits Reengineering requires a willingness to undergo critical self-analysis, to encounter change of the broadest and deepest kind, and to maintain the discipline required of a rigorous process. When approached with commitment, it can serve as a tool that fundamentally and permanently alters the competitive position of an organization enabling it to meet the new challenges it will face in the months and years ahead.

Immediate Internal Success Story When choosing the first processes to reengineer, the feasibility of accomplishing the project in a relatively short time period should be considered. If the first process reengineered takes a year to complete and is a long and difficult project, organizational support and commitment will be negatively affected.

A utility company we are working with found that after a year of trying to reengineer "world hunger" type issues the organization was convinced that process reengineering just would not work for them. Individuals involved in the effort were discouraged and frustrated. People not involved were convinced that this reengineering "stuff" was a waste of time and money. Some speculated that process reengineering only works in manufacturing companies. By providing a meaningful success story they learned how wrong they were. By carefully selecting a "real work" process that was clearly defined with a beginning and an end, had set boundary conditions, and the potential for high impact results over a short term, we were able to coach the reengineering team to totally reengineer the selected process. The real surprise was that the team completed its work over a three week period. The client's reengineering team, by carefully selecting and

Consequences to the Organization

reengineering a well defined "real work" process, not only successfully reengineered the process but revitalized the entire organization's reengineering effort and provided a model and process for success.

Organizational Culture

The organization needs to see relatively short term results - a critical internal success story - that enhances the commitment to and enthusiasm for the reengineering effort. It accomplishes an improved attitude toward change and decreases the amount of resistance that may be encountered. The internal success story sets the reengineering process apart from other improvement or training programs by letting everyone share in its success, increasing capacity in other areas of the organization, and improving business results.

As the reengineering effort picks up and more reengineering teams are created, a second level of benefits will appear. Employee commitment to teamwork will increase and more people will volunteer to work in teams. This not only helps the reengineering effort, but also improves the overall feeling of community and collective accomplishment that increases morale and commitment to the organization in its pursuit of change. Traditional mindsets and barriers regarding departments and functional jobs begin to be broken down and removed. Once these traditional behaviors and attitudes are removed, improvements in bottom line results begin to appear. Process speed increases, while failure rates decrease. Customer satisfaction rises due to the nature of the improved performance and general enthusiasm by at least one-third of the organization.

Consequences to the Organization

Rule of Thirds

When dealing with organizational change - particularly of this magnitude - it is normal to expect a certain amount of resistance to the reengineering effort. People who are committed to the way things are currently being run, no matter how effective or ineffective they may be, will be upset when asked to change.

But the important thing to remember about dealing with this resistance is that it cannot be allowed to hold the reengineering effort back. Reengineering efforts fail not because of resistance, but because the leaders of the movement did not provide clear and consistent visionary direction and leadership when confronted with the initial challenges to change.

Identifying resistance to change and determining how to address it can be described in a model called the "rule of thirds." Simply put, this rule suggests that when introducing a major change to an organization, after carefully communicating the change and educating employees, it will quickly be endorsed and embraced by approximately one-third of the organization. Another third will react negatively and resist the change for a variety of reasons. The middle third will remain overtly neutral, but will soon start to shift in the direction of the third that they believe is "winning" in the battle.

Consequences to the Organization

Making the Rule of Thirds Work

There is a clear method that will create the best response to this condition: place all your support, energy, resources and investment in the third supporting the change you seek to make. By giving them the time, the resources and the recognition, they will be successful in implementing the change. This will bring the middle third along, and pave the way for a strategy to address the resistant third.

Unfortunately, most leaders and managers unwittingly behave in just the opposite fashion. They place extraordinary effort in convincing and "winning over" the resistant third. By being recalcitrant or remaining skeptical, this third continues to receive the prime attention of management, leaving little or no time for the supporters of the change. The middle third sees that the resistant third is getting the attention, shifts in the negative direction, and the battle is lost.

One of our consultants recently coached a reengineering team of ten individuals representing a broad cross section from a manufacturing client. It was clear from the start that one of the team members thought this "whole reengineering work is a waste of time." The individual communicated his negative attitude through his comments and actions to the whole team. As often happens, the team carefully listened to the negative comments. At first, after the team realized that their teammate was "just plain negative," they tried to convince the person of some of the positive work and changes the team was achieving. But all their efforts could not overcome the individual's pessimistic and negative attitude. Finally in frustration, the team confronted the behavior and provided a face saving opportunity for

Consequences to the Organization

**Making the
Rule of Thirds
Work**

the person to stop participating as part of the team. The individual took advantage of the opportunity to leave and the positive work energy and forward momentum of the team dramatically increased. The message is clear. Support those who support your change initiative. They will create success and bring many others along with them.

If this strategy is effectively deployed, this leaves the remaining resistant third. What happens to them? Approximately half will shift in a positive direction as well when they see two-thirds of the organization moving toward the change. Of the remaining sixth, half of these will respond to direct feedback that resistance is no longer acceptable and that they must conform to the change if they are to continue to receive support in the organization.

In cases of severe resistance, the final twelfth may indeed choose to leave the organization. Research regarding major change indicates that this is approximately the turnover percentage (5-10%) that occurs in the twenty-four month period following major change - from both voluntary and involuntary actions.

Kurt Lewin, a prominent social scientist of this century, conducted extensive research regarding change and developed a very effective tool called the Force Field Analysis as a way of identifying the forces that are driving forward on behalf of change, and those resisting change. His research revealed that it is significantly more effective to remove the resisting forces than to increase the driving forces. If only the driving forces are increased, they may prevail but the resisting forces remain. They simply go

Consequences to the Organization

underground and wait for an opportunity to resurface. By removing the resisting forces, the driving forces already in place will shift the momentum, and increase the effectiveness and speed of the change.

Resistance to change is not necessarily a consequence of malicious behavior, ill intentions, or sabotage. It often comes from well intended individuals who may simply not understand the need for change; may need some education regarding the benefits of the change; or who may simply have a low personal tolerance for change.

Resistance should be treated with understanding and sensitivity. The goal is not to overcome those who resist but to win them over.

Chapter Two

The Role of Leadership

Leadership Defined in the New Business Environment

The Challenge

In this changing world, transformational change, and more specifically reengineering, is a tool for revitalizing organizations. What kind of skills and behaviors are needed to lead an organization through this turbulent era of radical change? The traditional view of leaders as authoritarian, "take charge" directors, no longer works in this global economy where problems facing organizations are much more complex. The interdependencies of all aspects of the organization; the increased span of professional knowledgeable workers; the flattening of the organizational hierarchy; and the widespread availability of information due to technology are only some of the factors that make it virtually impossible for any one person to serve as the fountain of wisdom, truth, and decision-making for an organization. On the following page are some of the internal and external factors that require a new kind of leadership.

Transactional Management - The Traditional Industrial Model

The traditional definition of managing is to bring about; to accomplish; to have charge of or responsibility for; to conduct. Management functions were often used interchangeably with leadership. However, a focus on transactional management and short term tasks does not meet the criteria for leadership today. Transactional management is largely about supporting day-to-day steady state functions. The focus is on achieving short term goals with ever increasing efficiency. Stability and predictability describe the desired condition. From this context, change is bad and infers that something is "wrong." Transactional managers will often seek to contain or accommodate change, or try to "keep it under control."

Leadership Defined in the New Business Environment

The
Challenge

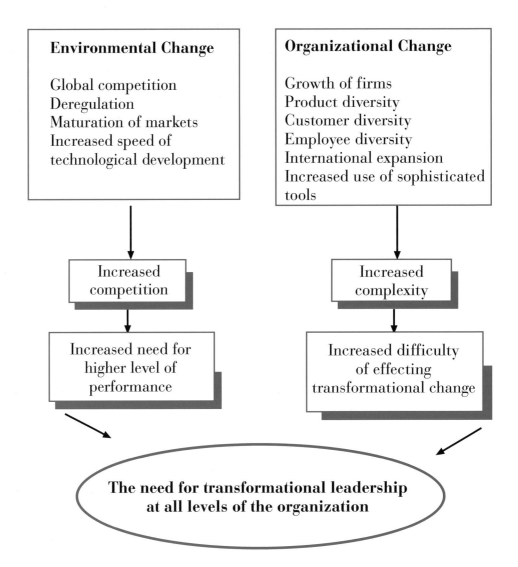

Leadership Defined in the New Business Environment

Transformational Leadership

If we accept the new definition of leadership as setting vision and direction; creating organizational alignment; and determining resource deployment, then transactional management is not sufficient. A different type of leadership is required to move organizations through transformation and reengineering efforts. Transformational change requires shifts in behavior for leaders, managers, employees, and functional organizations. Transformational leaders view change as an opportunity and a necessity, and strive to support organizational systems that search for purposeful changes. They provide the vision and direction for the company in their quest for change, addressing economic, organizational, and human issues.

Goals of Transformational Leadership

The aim of transformational leadership is to "transform" people, processes, and organizations in a way that empowers them to attain the common vision and goals of the organization from a position of personal commitment. Empowerment:

- Enlarges vision and understanding
- Clarifies purpose in activities
- Brings behavior into line with values, goals and strategies
- Brings about changes that are self-generating, permanent, and momentum-building

Transformational leadership empowers individuals and teams within an organization to make personal and process changes through reengineering and process improvement. This empowerment develops commitment to the larger organizational vision and enables people to feel that they are capable of striving for and achieving the goals to which they are collectively committed.

Leadership Defined in the New Business Environment

Transactional Management	Transformational Leadership
• Emphasis on short term - get the job done	• Oriented toward meeting long term goals in accordance with overriding principles
• Focus on tactical issues	• Focus on missions and strategies for achieving results
• Concerned with position, policies, procedures	• Build on need for meaning and cooperation
• Focus on supervision, control, conformance	• Focus on feedback and responsibility
• Look for compliance	• Aim for commitment
• Follow role expectations within current system	• Design and redesign jobs, roles and processes to meet challenges
• Support structures and systems that maximize efficiency and guarantee short term profits	• Develop flexibility in structures and systems to promote periodic evaluation of effectiveness
Outcome: *Order and predictability*	**Outcome:** *Transformational change*

Leadership Defined in the New Business Environment

Role of the Transformational Leader

In this new business model, what does the transformational leader do? First, the leader must establish the direction of the organization and of the core processes within that organization. This is done through the development of a vision of the future and working with a core leadership team to create strategies necessary for achieving that vision.

The second element of the leader's role involves creating alignment throughout the organization. By sharing the vision with all employees and stressing the need for change, leaders demonstrate their personal commitment to improvement and obtain the commitment of others. This commitment is dependent on everyone understanding the vision and the strategies that support them. In this way, transformational leaders build an infrastructure, or a coalition of forces, that achieve the vision.

The third role of the transformational leader is deployment. This involves motivating and inspiring people to overcome resistance to change by mobilizing the energy and commitment to achieve the vision. Transformational leaders focus on the positive - those people who are firmly committed to achieving the agenda and, through this reinforcement, can build an ever expanding coalition among others who were previously neutral. In all organizations there is the need for balance - the integration of effective management with effective leadership. When reengineered, this balance is especially vital.

Leadership Styles

Leadership and Change

The following chart shows the variations of balance between management and leadership. As indicated, conditions of high change and high organizational complexity require significant contributions from both management and leadership. Since this text is devoted to the role of leadership and teams in the high change environment of reengineering, the focus of this section is to address the leadership side of the equation.

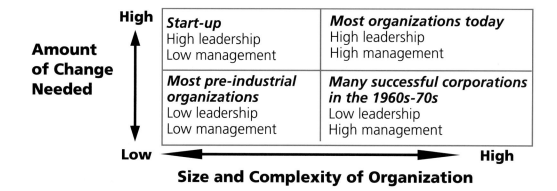

Leadership and Organizational Culture

Culture is increasingly recognized as a vital aspect of the health of an organization. A number of key elements of culture have already been defined in the context of vision and the environment needed to support a reengineering change effort. Because of its criticality, some additional attention should be paid to this matter.

Culture is the manifestation of the core values, hidden assumptions or beliefs governing the organization, and its tangible artifacts (systems, policies, procedures, etc.).

Leadership Styles

In order for major change to be effective in creating the type of organization described in the first section of this book, leaders must create a culture conducive to high degrees of empowerment, participation, and collaboration.

Creating such a culture is accomplished through four key actions:

1. The leader must personally exemplify and serve as a role model for the desired culture and demand the same behavior from the rest of the senior leadership team.

2. The desired culture must be clearly articulated through the vision, mission, core values, and guiding principles of the organization.

3. The organizational structure, systems, processes, policies, reward systems, and tools must be in alignment with the desired culture and value system.

4. The entire leadership and management structure must exemplify and demand the behaviors that reflect the desired culture - at all levels and under all circumstances and conditions.

Leadership Styles

What is the style that leadership must demonstrate to create the conditions essential for a positive reengineering environment? The answer does not lie in simple responses such as authoritarian or participative behaviors. Nor is it exemplified by modeling individuals such as popular political, military, or industrial leaders.

Leadership Styles

**Leadership
Styles**

A wide variety of interpersonal behaviors can be effective in a leadership capacity as long as they are driven by a core set of values and guiding principles. These principles reflect a fundamental shift from the industrial model described previously. Recently the president of a very successful nationally based insurance company said his job was to "model the coaching, counseling, mentoring leadership style we preach about." He went on to say "If I, as the most visible organizational leader, do not walk the talk, how can I expect anyone else to?". While not complete, the following list is a description of the behavioral shifts that exemplify the leadership style needed to support transformational change and reengineering in a team-based environment.

1. *From "command and control" to stewardship*
   Leaders must guide, support, and sponsor individuals, teams and processes rather than serve as directors and controllers of events and circumstances.

2. *From decision-maker to consensus builder*
   Decisions developed through consensus invite participation and build commitment through the decision-making process.

3. *From task to process focus*
   Traditional leaders focus on tasks and activities, and guide them by using a command and control style. Transformational leaders focus on processes - ensuring their ability to meet customer requirements and fidelity in use.

Leadership Styles

4. *From transactional focus to transformational guidance*
   Guidance for change and support for the ambiguity and risk inherent in a changing environment.

5. *From tactical to strategic orientation*
   Strategic focus must keep the marketplace and customer in the forefront with an emphasis on the long term impact of decisions and actions.

6. *From individual to team orientation*
   Performance and success are achieved through team behavior with an emphasis on collaboration and synergistic results.

7. *From control to participation*
   Listening skills, along with facilitation and involvement, are hallmarks of this shift in style.

8. *From power to empowerment*
   Sharing power with others, enabling and encouraging others to act with courage and independence are integral to a reengineering context.

Empowerment Empowerment is a concept that is used and misunderstood with great frequency. A traditional interpretation of empowerment comes from the classical organizational understanding of its root word: power. Power in the classical sense has to do with the ability to impose a position on others or on the circumstances. Position power carries with it the authority to commit resources; spend money; assign individuals; and make decisions.

Leadership Styles

Empowerment   Personal power includes the force of will to cause others to act as you would like. When individuals or teams are told that they are to be empowered, they often respond from this traditional understanding of power. Questions such as: "What is our signature authority?" or "How much budget do we now control?" or "Can we now tell or direct others what to do?" are classical manifestations of the perception that empowerment is the transfer of formal power from someone else to the newly empowered person or team.

This is not empowerment; it is delegation of formal authority.

The new business environment requires a new meaning for the concept of power. Power in the broader sense is the ability to influence others and cause them to change their behavior. If this book causes you, the reader, to shift some of your thinking and act differently, then this book has had a powerful effect on you. And we, the consultants, have had a powerful impact on your life without ever having met you. This is a different concept of power: the ability to influence others and potentially cause them to make decisions, select courses of action, or change their behaviors. It has nothing to do with formal hierarchy, authority, or control.

Empowerment provides the opportunity to potentially influence the course of events for others. If the reengineering team is properly authorized to redesign a process, and present its recommendations to others for endorsement, it has been given a pathway by which it may change the course of action for that organization. It has been empowered and with

Leadership Styles

that empowerment comes the freedom to act, limited only by the boundaries of its charter as a team.

Empowerment defined in this context creates a high degree of freedom of action, an invitation to take risks, the opportunity to be innovative, and welcomes full participation.

Leadership is the act of creating organizational vision, alignment and deployment. When implemented with a style similar to the one described above with the intention of creating a team-based culture, it has the potential of nurturing an environment that will enable reengineering and organizational change to thrive.

Leadership and Timing

Importance and Urgency

Reengineering is generally treated as both a "high importance" and "high urgency" initiative by an organization. There are several reasons for the deep sense of urgency that surrounds this effort.

First, it usually takes an organization a fair amount of time to come to the conclusion that it needs to take an aggressive improvement initiative, and that reengineering of its core business processes is the best undertaking. Many factors can slow the process down. Reengineering requires that the senior leadership team be in full alignment with this effort before the really serious work gets underway. Very often a committee has been assigned the task of studying and benchmarking other reengineering initiatives prior to making a decision. There may have been a consultant review process that took several months. Some members of the senior leadership team may have been in disagreement and needed to be brought together before the work could be carried any further. Other pressing business matters - budget, strategic planning, new product launch, relocation, downsizing, etc.- may have to have been completed first to create the room for this effort. There may have been a significant internal search for the right person, or the right team, to guide this effort and then to create the availability for that person. For these or any other number of reasons, there is usually a build-up of anticipation prior to the actual launch of the reengineering effort. During this period there is a sense of both anticipation and expectation that starts to develop among the senior leadership team, if not throughout the organization.

Leadership and Timing

Therefore, the reengineering team is typically "behind the power curve" from the first day of its team chartering. This adds to the sense of urgency and pressure throughout the initiative.

In addition, most organizations lack a full appreciation of the requirements and benefits of a participatory process. We tend to be so task driven that we push for results and often "brute force" conclusions and decisions by throwing more resources at the issue at hand.

However, reengineering is a process that requires the full knowledge and participation of all the key individuals and functional groups involved in the process. The success of most reengineering efforts lies not in the elegance of the solution but in the ability of the organization to accept, install and then apply the recommendations. This requires both involvement and participation throughout the process.

Sustaining Momentum

Understanding the timing requirements is critical. In the early stages of the process, it may not appear that much is happening. Teams may be meeting, resources are being consumed, activity levels are high, availability for other efforts is reduced, but results are not yet flowing. This is the first danger period. There will be pressures from well-intended individuals to divert some of these resources to other more urgent matters that were initially unanticipated when the reengineering resources were committed. There may be pressures as well from other individuals who are not convinced that reengineering is the right approach or who are resistant to change to show that "this effort isn't working" and to kill it in its seminal stages.

Leadership and Timing

Sustaining Momentum

Senior leadership must be aware of these pressures at this stage of the process and stay the course. Resources must be maintained, support continued, and active interest and participation sustained. The initiative must not be allowed to be eroded and destroyed with death by a thousand cuts.

This is the first timing concern and may continue for some number of months.

Installation Through Participation

The second timing threat occurs when recommendations have been made and endorsed, and the installation process is getting underway. At this point there is great pressure to "push" the solution and enforce immediate and widespread use of the newly engineered process. This is the second major window of caution.

Change does not occur simply because leadership wills it, wants it or commands it. It must be installed with the participation of those who use it every day. This installation requires a period of trial use so that many people can touch the new process, try it out, see how it improves performance and then start to use it because "they said so"; not because "someone else said so."

Some reengineered processes may not have this luxury. Major technology-based conversions may require a "switch-over" day. If this is the case, then adequate communication, education, pilot testing and preparation is essential.

Leadership and Timing

In cases where the new process is replacing the old without a total immediate conversion, it is best if the new process can be used, tested, validated, and then be accepted and gradually sweep through the organization. Our experience has shown that the greatest success occurs when there is a demand pull for the improved process rather than a management push.

The clear message, however, is the same. Major change requires time. Time for design; time for development; time for installation; time for practice; and time for acceptance. This timing cycle must be built into the plan and senior leadership must guide the acceptance and installation process. Many excellent initiatives have failed because they were killed prior to having a fair chance and time to prove their effectiveness. Consistent support and an understanding of the time for system installation, acceptance and process restabilization is essential for the success of a major reengineering initiative.

Creating the Shared Vision

The Vision as a Driving Force

Reengineering should not be considered until the organization has clearly defined its vision or desired future. Vision statements vary widely in length, format, and levels of specificity. The common property that they must share, however, is a clarity about the desired organizational future state. This picture should be developed through the process of participation and consensus among senior management; and contain sufficient clarity so that the vision can be translated into aligned action at all levels of the organization. In order to achieve this level of clarity, vision statements are often accompanied by missions, core values, and guiding principles. They may also be accompanied by strategic direction, goals, priorities, critical success factors, and measures.

The guiding principle for the use of a vision for reengineering is: the greater the clarity, the better. It is much easier to hit a well defined and marked target than a general statement of "improved market positioning" or "increased global competitiveness." Once the vision is defined, the reengineering team has a clear picture of the objectives of both the organization and of the reengineering effort, and can be more focused in its work.

Energy from a Shared Vision

Visions should be exhilarating. They create the spark and the excitement that lifts the organization out of the mundane. In a corporation, a shared vision changes people's relationship with the company. It is no longer management's company, it becomes "our" company. A shared vision is the first step in creating the environment for people who mistrusted each other to begin to work together toward a common purpose. In the presence of

Creating the Shared Vision

greatness, pettiness disappears. In the absence of a great dream, pettiness often prevails.

The existence of an organizational vision, no matter how strategically sound and uplifting, ceases to have the unifying and focusing result necessary for reaching that future state if not effectively communicated and shared with everyone in the organization. Many leaders under-estimate the continuous and vital effort required to maintain and execute a communication strategy designed to make the vision a shared and viable strategic force for the employees of the organization.

Shared visions foster risk-taking and experimentation. They compel courage so naturally that people don't even realize the extent of their courage. Courage simply becomes whatever is needed in pursuit of the vision.

A leader of a 1,000 person Division of a Fortune 500 Company shared with one of our consultants how odd it felt sharing her vision. "It felt so strange, I deeply and personally believe in our vision, but the first time I shared it with a group of 30 or 40 employees, I almost stopped midway through the discussion. As I listened to my own words, presenting what the vision meant to me, I thought this sounds like motherhood and apple pie. These people are going to think I am really corny. But then I looked at the group. They were paying very close attention, over half were nodding their heads. I could feel their energy and buy in. At that moment I realized how incredibly powerful a shared vision can be."

Creating the Shared Vision

Energy from a Shared Vision

A learning organization cannot exist without shared vision. Without a pull toward some goal that a committed group of people truly wants to achieve, the forces in support of the status quo will likely be overwhelming.

Shared vision addresses one of the primary questions that has often thwarted efforts to develop strategic thinking in management: "How can a commitment to the long term be fostered?" In every instance where one finds a long term view actually operating in human affairs, there is a long term vision at work.

A vision for an organization answers the basic question, "What is the future that our business strives to attain?" This leads to serious thinking on everyone's part, and a necessity for a total commitment to the vision. This commitment is easily achieved when a vision successfully creates a picture of the future around which people can identify, and take personal action. The vision must be clear enough to set direction, but broad enough so that everyone can take personal meaning from it. Employees can comply with a vision set by senior leaders, but the purpose of a good vision is to get people to commit to and enroll in its message.

Creating the Shared Vision

Committing to a Shared Vision

How can leaders achieve this commitment and enrollment?

1. Be enrolled themselves. There is no point attempting to encourage another to be enrolled when you are not. This is selling, not enrolling, and will at best produce superficial agreement and compliance. At worst, it will sow the seeds for future resentment.

2. Be on the level. Describe the vision as simply and honestly as possible.

3. Allow time for employees to choose to become enrolled on their own terms. If employees sense honesty and commitment from leaders, they are quite likely to make the enrollment choice.

Commitment feels like:

- Being invited to participate - an honor or a privilege
- Having a purposeful drive toward goals and results
- Being clearly aligned to organizational goals
- An essential component of personal success
- A tool for improving the quality of each individual's work
- Collaboration through a team effort

Creating the Shared Vision

Visions Specific to the Reengineering Effort

Once the organization is clear and committed to its core vision, a specific vision for the reengineering effort should be created. After a process has been chosen for reengineering, a vision describing its purpose must be developed. This is critical for focusing the reengineering team on the goal. This vision must then be communicated through the entire organization to achieve commitment to the reengineering effort and the changes that will ensue.

Creating a process vision series as a vital linkage between the organization's overall strategic direction and the process to be reengineered. Business processes are the means by which strategic goals are realized and work is produced. Without effective alignment between process and strategy, meeting the future state prescribed by the strategic thinking process becomes endangered. The importance of producing a viable process vision for the reengineering effort, consisting of measurable objectives and characteristics that inspire commitment and action, is critical to the initiative's success.

A reengineering process vision should indeed be "visionary" in the sense that it sets adventurous, tough, and challenging targets to meet while radically altering the paradigms embedded in the current process. A process vision that "rationalizes" or "simplifies" a process without shifting the underlying thinking about how the work is achieved will accomplish little in moving the organization toward meaningful business results. Creating a process vision is a balance between inspiration, creativity and measurable targets. Reengineering can cause a company to reassess its overall strategic

Creating the Shared Vision

position. Understanding this as a possible consequence of the "visioning" process in reengineering cannot be ignored.

The responsibility for creating the process vision in most cases falls upon the Steering Team, but can be revised after the more "micro" and complex work of reengineering teams has taken place. There are six key stages in developing or refining a process vision:

1. Assessing current organizational strategy
2. Acquiring and understanding critical process customer requirements
3. Benchmarking similar processes
4. Developing the vision elements
5. Developing specific process characteristics
6. Developing the critical success factors for the process

The graphic on the next page maps out the specific approach to creating a process vision. The model distinguishes between process objectives, which are measurable or quantifiable, and process characteristics which, although just as vital, are measurable only in a qualitative way. These combine to bring achievability to the vision. The more specific the process vision, the more likely the reengineering teams will achieve the radical redesigns required for the organizational repositioning. Steps in process visioning should move toward greater specificity, and employ analysis of respective categories such as: process flow, output, internal and external organizational aspects, cost, cycle time, quality, people, technologies, structural systems,

Creating the Shared Vision

**Visions
Specific
to the
Reengineering
Effort**

and critical interfaces. The successful process vision provides the reengineering teams with the necessary goal drivers and "stretch" goals to achieve radical process redesign.

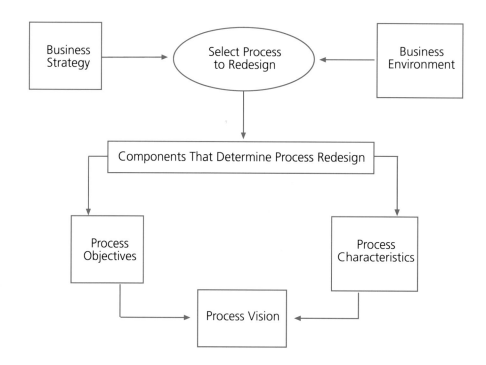

Shared Responsibility

The Traditional View of Responsibility

Responsibility is a cornerstone of organizational life. Defining individual responsibility creates role clarity, establishes accountability, and eliminates the potential for chaos and unproductive conflict.

In a traditional context, responsibilities are largely an individual matter. When an individual is assigned a responsibility, he or she is personally accountable for generating the results expected for the defined area. Typically, responsibilities are measurable, individual, defined, tied to accountability, and form the basis for recognition and reward systems.

The emphasis on individual responsibility is paradoxically the dilemma that can be the source of confusion and conflict among teams. When teams are formed, they often divide up the work they are expected to do, and then assign individual responsibility and accountability to the team members for their respective elements of the work.

A team assigned to implement a sales order process, for example, might give one person the responsibility for inputting the data, another for processing it, a third the responsibility for addressing customer issues, etc.

This system is adequate as long as the work is going well and no major changes are required. However when problems arise, there is a tendency for each individual to protect his/her personal area of responsibility, assigning the blame or fault to others. No one seems to "own" the entire scope of the work.

Shared Responsibility

Primary and Secondary Responsibility

As organizations recognize the interdependence of work and the necessity for teams to work together, individual responsibility becomes a barrier as well as an asset. A step toward addressing this issue is the concept of primary and secondary responsibility. In this context, each individual has his/her personal primary responsibility. In addition, each individual has a secondary responsibility for the work of others involved in similar or related processes or tasks.

Secondary responsibility means that the individual should be available to provide support as required to help colleagues and teammates. However, each individual must attend to the primary responsibilities as the first order of business. How else could they be primary?

While the concept of mutual support through secondary responsibilities does start to build a broader sense of community, it still divides the work pie into its elements, and supports discrete and independent action rather than a fully interdependent environment.

Shared Responsibility

The concept of shared responsibility expands these ideas further and is designed to build full team interdependence and collective effort. Individuals still have their areas of personal primary responsibility. However, they also have a shared responsibility for the success of the entire enterprise, process, team, or work product of which they are a part. This means that the failure of any individual member of the team represents the failure of the entire team. There is nothing less.

Shared Responsibility

Under these circumstances, commitment to the task must also mean commitment to the other members of the team. If any team member fails, the work of the entire team is jeopardized and everyone shares in the total and shared responsibility for team performance and success.

Shared responsibility often creates initial anxiety and concern. Each individual now realizes that the performance of others directly impacts personal performance. When fully developed in a team environment, shared responsibility is not only comfortable for all the team members, it is essential to the creation of high performance teams.

One word of caution regarding shared responsibility is in order. When an organization makes the commitment to shared responsibility it is making the commitment to a team-based work environment. In order to fully implement this concept, the reward and recognition systems of the organization must be brought into alignment. Shared responsibility requires team-based reward and recognition systems in addition to individual-based performance systems. It also leads to the demand for some risk-based compensation systems. Such shifts must be studied carefully to identify both their intended and unintended systemic consequences. When developed with careful thought and design, they have the potential to create extraordinary shifts in performance.

Supporting the Process Through Sponsorship and Process Ownership

Sponsorship

Organizational change on the scale and intensity of reengineering a core business process must be sponsored by a senior executive within the organization. Due to most organizational structures consisting of functional units, one single sponsor, no matter how senior in the organization, is often not adequate to ensure the success of the initiative. A core business process that flows across organizational functions requires the sponsorship of all the functional leaders involved, as well as the corporate executive team.

In any major transformational change, specific roles can get confused; understanding and clarifying these roles is vital.

The *advocate* is one who proposes the change. This role may be assumed by a senior management team member, a functional head, or the president.

The role of *change agent* is fulfilled by the reengineering teams and process owners responsible for implementing the changes.

The role of *sponsor* is best defined as the person who serves as the ombudsman for the change and champions the reengineering initiative. The steering team may contain one or more senior managers who actively sponsor the reengineering effort. If the CEO or President is the most appropriate sponsor, but chooses not to be actively involved, he may well thwart the initiative unintentionally. Beware of the trap of the CEO who, although championing the reengineering effort, appoints an inappropriate

Supporting the Process Through Sponsorship and Process Ownership

sponsor below him or her. Reengineering sponsorship is critical at the most senior level in an organization. It tests the limits of the organization and requires the support that can elicit commitment for the changes at the executive team level, and release much needed resources. As a team of executive clients recently experienced, the results of the reengineering team they had sponsored and chartered caused them to examine their own leadership style. They found that as the organization transformed and became more empowering they too needed to individually and collectively change their style to support transformation and empowerment. In the end, the senior management team must endorse a change or expansion in the boundary conditions.

Many organizations that initiate the steps required to undergo major transformational change have not thoroughly considered the role of process ownership. Frequently they have not identified process owners at all. The common silo or "stove pipe" structure of many organizations supports process ownership only within functional areas. There is rarely a process owner who crosses the functional boundaries to serve as the steward for the overall process. Functional "process owners" are clearly critical members of the steering team or the reengineering teams. They are not adequately positioned within the organization to act as sponsors unless one has been assigned the ownership role for the entire process.

Supporting the Process Through Sponsorship and Process Ownership

**Process
Ownership**

Redesigning a core business process sets in motion changes not explicit in the actual redesign of the process: the need for changes in organizational behavior; application and management of alternative technologies; transformation of existing work structures; and development of very different skills around process management and process ownership.

As discussed, most process ownership is incorrectly applied and defined around functional authority. An order fulfillment process crosses many functional lines, and in traditionally structured organizations ownership occurs only at the part of the process that crosses into a specific functional area. No overall process owner exists. For this reason, clearly defined process ownership should be decided prior to reengineering taking place.

A vital part of successful reengineering is unfreezing the power structure around functional ownership. If this behavioral change is not addressed early in the process, the strongly embedded behaviors around functional ownership may cause divisiveness and destructive power plays during the redesign, and endanger its success. The make-up of the reengineering team plays a key role in beginning to break down territorial insularity by ensuring appropriate cross-functional and geographic representation on the teams. This in turn allows freedom for the reengineering teams to develop effective cross-functional and seamless process redesign.

Educating and developing appropriate leadership behaviors to make broad cross-functional ownership of the new core business process possible should not be ignored.

Chapter Three

The Role of Teams in
Business Process Reengineering

The Role of Teams

Introduction

Most leaders in today's business world have chartered and developed many teams of varying types and with varying degrees of empowerment. They have come to realize the crucial role of teams in offering flexibility, responsiveness and quality service to customers. Reengineering a core business process demands a team approach because of the extensive nature of the project, and the importance of bringing together multiple perspectives, talents and experience with the process. A team effort is vital for effective analysis and redesign.

The objective of business process reengineering is to significantly improve the business performance of the organization as a whole. This increased process focus may result in a changed culture including the shifting of the control of work from supervisors to self-directed teams. The actual reengineering process itself also requires effective team management. This is best achieved by forming three different types of teams: a steering team, reengineering teams, and process implementation teams.

The Steering Team

The steering team oversees the whole reengineering effort and is usually the senior leadership of the organization. Although most senior leadership groups call themselves a team, in actuality they frequently behave more like a committee. Independent functional goals, cross-functional conflict, resource scarcity, and lack of a shared vision and collective accountability are some of the factors that detract from team behavior and performance. In addition, the career paths of most executives call for robust individualism and sophisticated political behavioral characteristics that can destroy true teamwork.

The Role of Teams

The Steering Team

The challenge for these executives in the steering team is to work together and create output that is "greater than the sum of its individual parts." This must be addressed if the reengineering effort is to receive the necessary leadership for success. We have found that reengineering may well be the catalyst for helping the executive level group become a true team. The results of this team development pay substantial dividends even after the reengineering process is completed.

The Reengineering Team

The reengineering team(s) conduct the process analysis and process redesign work. Due to the scope of the effort required in reengineering a major core business process, several reengineering teams may need to be formed to address all aspects of a macro business process. Attempting to reengineer a major process with one single team could require so much representation and be so large that it could not work effectively as a team. In addition, the skill level requirements might be too diverse for optimal cross-functional input into the new process design. The advantage of multiple reengineering teams is derived not only in more effective team performance but by each team having a sufficiently manageable scope to focus in sufficient depth on its process issues.

The Implementation Team

The process implementation teams are responsible for installing the reengineered process and ensuring its success throughout the operational level of the organization. These implementation teams may be the reengineering teams rechartered to a new role, or they may include some reengineering team members and other new members as well. It is possible, but not likely, that it is an entirely different set of individuals.

The Role of Teams

Cross-functional membership in these teams is essential. The cross-functional expertise used in reengineering the process is crucial to effective implementation. These teams may face resistance from traditional functional structures and will need to be supported by the steering team. It is surprising how many "turf" issues still prevail in organizations even after core process management and ownership have been introduced.

The Structural Relationship of the Teams

The structural relationship of these teams is outlined in the diagram below.

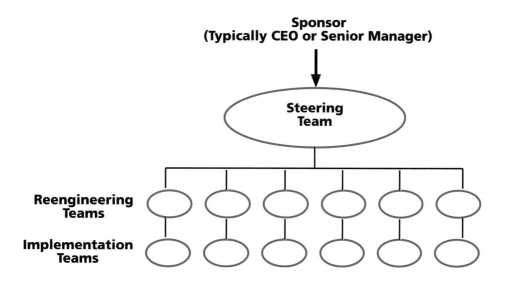

The Role of Teams

Creating the Reengineering Vision

The specific expectations and goals to be achieved from the reengineering effort are crystallized during the vision setting process. Vision setting is first conducted with the steering team to create the picture of the desired state at the end of the process. Depending on needs, the vision setting process may include a mission, goals, critical success factors, boundary conditions and measurements. These vision elements are shared with the reengineering team. They should continue to be retested and validated or modified as the reengineering teams assess the organizational and marketplace enablers and constraints affecting the process. The ability to successfully measure the elements and attributes of the vision drive both the redesign and the capability of monitoring the redesigned process. The ongoing monitoring of the redesign throughout implementation enables the reengineering teams to adjust and change elements throughout the process.

The role of the steering team in communicating and building alignment of all aspects of the vision with the reengineering teams is vital for success and is part of the chartering process. The critical success factors play a crucial role in focusing the reengineering teams and ensuring the necessary alignment between the redesign and the organizational strategy.

Setting Boundary Conditions

Prior to chartering the reengineering teams, the steering team develops the broad parameters within which the reengineering initiative will be conducted. Boundaries need to be drawn around the available resources and technologies; the expected time-frame for the reengineering effort; assurances of how ongoing business will continue to be delivered; specific organizational areas that are fair game or out-of-bounds for the

The Role of Teams

reengineering teams; and areas that would require prior consultation and agreement if they are to be impacted. These "boundary conditions" should not be rigid or too narrow. The steering team must define the "what" of the reengineering process but not the "how." This is the domain of the reengineering teams.

The boundary conditions are set to maintain an overall organizational check and balance mechanism. They should be communicated as guidelines for the reengineering teams rather than rigid demarcations or forbidden territory that they enter at their peril. Sensitivity in setting the boundary conditions is critical to ensure that the reengineering teams feel empowered to exercise their responsibilities outside current process paradigms and employ a high level of creativity and freedom.

Recently, an executive level "reengineering steering committee" that we were coaching developed eighteen boundary conditions for a process reengineering team they were going to charter. The steering committee's coach was able to point out that the eighteen boundary conditions in effect limited and literally predetermined the results that would come from the reengineering efforts. By examining and challenging the perceptions and mental models that surrounded the boundary conditions, the steering committee became very comfortable in reducing the number from eighteen to five. The result was that the final five boundary conditions defined a wide playing field for the reengineering team and empowered them to truly reengineer the identified processes.

The Role of Teams

Setting Boundary Conditions

By requesting specific membership representation across the organization in the reengineering teams, the steering team can ensure that both the skills and perspectives from all appropriate organizational areas are represented. This is their best tool for the preventive elimination of the potential for bias in the process redesign.

The Steering Team

Introduction

It is very difficult for a reengineering effort to succeed without an effective steering team responsible for the overall leadership, coordination and resource allocation for the core business process redesign. Steering team membership typically includes senior executives or key management from across the organization whose functional responsibilities are affected directly or indirectly by the process to be reengineered. The importance of this team holding high level authority is critical if the initiative is to receive the appropriate cross-functional direction and resources it may need.

The organizational structure, nature of its industry, and the core business process being reengineered will determine the essential senior management membership of the steering team. Due to the widespread impact that process reengineering has throughout the organization, all key areas of the business may well be represented on the steering team.

Responsibilities

Initially, the steering team is responsible for identifying the core process; establishing the process vision and undertaking appropriate high level benchmarking studies; determining the process critical success factors and measures; and defining the process boundary conditions. The steering team then develops the blueprint for how the reengineering teams will be structured through the reengineering process. This should be discussed and agreed with these teams in the team chartering process. Structure includes how the teams will be organized during the diagnosis phase, how they will communicate and share information with each other, and how they will ensure seamless work in the design phase.

The Steering Team

Responsibilities Effective leadership requires a concurrent organizational communication strategy that is both informative and candid about the potential implications of reengineering, along with maintaining communications of the status of progress and achievements. Many senior managers underestimate the importance of the continual communication needs throughout the organization. In a time of transformational change, it is even more critical to prepare employees and maintain the organizational commitment to the changes required by the process vision.

Sponsorship Each reengineering team should be sponsored by one appropriate member of the steering team. Steering team member selection as sponsors for a reengineering team should be made by matching knowledge and management responsibility on the steering team with the process area for which the reengineering team takes accountability.

Criteria for Success Following are the criteria essential for an effective steering team:

- Collective organizational authority regarding the business process to be reengineered.

- The commitment by every steering team member to the goals and consequences of the reengineering effort.

- The willingness and ability of steering team members to expand beyond their established individual roles and work as an effective cross-functional team providing the leadership for the collective company reengineering vision.

The Steering Team

- The ability and willingness to provide continuous communication to the organization of the reengineering vision; ongoing progress reports; results and successes; and solicit and respond to feedback from the organization regarding the reengineering effort.

- Maintaining an open and participative relationship with the reengineering teams.

Selection of Reengineering Team Members

The steering team's responsibility for chartering the reengineering team is pivotal. Before this can occur, team members must be chosen. One method for accomplishing this is for the steering team to pick the members directly. Another approach is to appoint team leaders for each team and have them choose their team members with the approval of the steering team.

The choice of membership is based on specific criteria, such as the following:

- Understanding of the broader business context requiring the reengineering initiative

- Technical skill set - this must meet the technical process needs of each reengineering team's redesign purpose

- Representation to provide adequate cross-functional expertise

- A willingness and openness to creative and alternative approaches to process redesign

- Previous experience working in teams

- Commitment to the reengineering effort

The Reengineering and Implementation Teams

Membership

The reengineering and implementation team leaders should have proven team leadership skills as well as the ability to meet the core criteria for team membership. A team leader should also have a high level of expertise in the specific process area to be reengineered and a breadth of knowledge and experience about the broader business unit. Each team leader is also the boundary manager between his/her team and the other teams providing the vital linkages and data to ensure value added seamless work for the overall process design. Finally, the team leader must be an effective communicator with the steering team.

The choice of team members for the reengineering or implementation team will be governed largely by the area of the core business process to be reengineered. Since activities at any point in a process impact the activities throughout the process, team members must be selected from all key points and interfaces throughout the process. This ensures both knowledge of the total process and the multiple perspectives that are developed at different points along the way. The figure on the following page depicts how, using a typical order fulfillment process as an example, the team might be identified and cross-functional membership derived.

The Reengineering and Implementation Teams

The Current Order Fulfillment Process

Functions and Departments

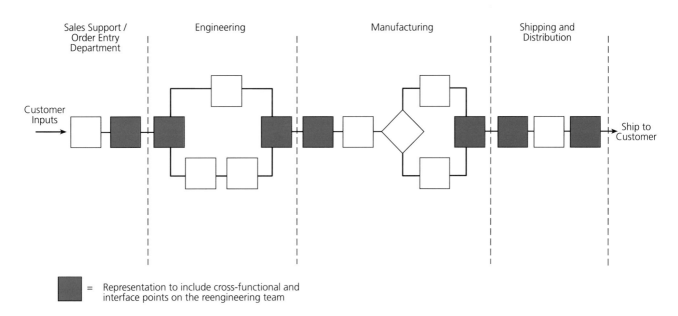

■ = Representation to include cross-functional and
        interface points on the reengineering team

The Reengineering Team

Customer Involvement

Most organizations would agree that reengineering without customer input runs counter to the principles of process reengineering. Therefore, it is recommended that at least one representative of the external customer group be included as a member of the reengineering team.

Companies tend to be very cautious about bringing customers into the internal mechanisms of their organization, especially at times of extensive change when the organization is perceived to be highly exposed. If the customer is one with whom the organization has had a successful, long term relationship and whose business volume is substantial, then it is recommended that this customer be solicited for direct and full reengineering team membership. The criteria for the individual to be selected from within the customer organization should be based on the extent of the individual's knowledge of the use, function and impact of the product or service. This is essential to provide the vital perspective to enhance the new process design. This individual should also have had previous team experience as well as being committed to the reengineering effort from the customer's point of view. The team must also continue to seek other customer input and not rely solely on the external customer on the team.

Many executives fear what they perceive to be exposure to customers of the company's underbelly during a period of transformational change. Indeed most customer organizations know you better than you know yourself, and would welcome the ability to form an alliance with a key supplier. The value to them is their ability to enhance your capability in meeting or exceeding their requirements. Where such participation has occurred, it

The Reengineering Team

has typically strengthened the business relationship between the two organizations and provided detailed customer design criteria for the newly reengineered process.

Critical Functions

The reengineering team performs the following: detailed process information gathering and analysis; detailed process redesign work; pilot testing and final process design; and implementation planning. These activities are detailed in the reengineering model and form the core work performed in any reengineering effort.

Team Structures

The structures used to perform the critical functions of the individual reengineering teams are not necessarily identical. There are several approaches to the coordination of the various reengineering teams. One approach is to have just one or a select few reengineering teams concentrate on the beginning reengineering stages. They perform the majority of the diagnostic work and synthesize their findings for other teams who will perform the detailed process design work, utilizing the work of the initial teams to guide their designs. This approach is well suited to an organization where restricted availability of human resources is a factor in the reengineering process.

Another approach is to divide the broader process into segments and have each team perform the full diagnosis and design for its segment. While efficient, this model presents the challenge of managing the "seams" between teams. It may also miss the broad overview perspective required for the real "breakthrough thinking" regarding the process at a higher level.

The Reengineering Team

**Team
Structures**

A third approach is to establish one initial reengineering team that conducts the diagnosis and then does the overall "high level" design. This design captures the potential breakthrough approaches. This team then identifies an appropriate number of sub-teams working under its direction to conduct the detailed design work for various stages of the process, while managing the "seams" between these teams.

This approach can be a bit more hierarchical and does demand a great deal of time and effort on the part of the overall team. However, because of the conceptual wholeness of the diagnosis and design stage, along with the greater integration across teams, it is the model most recommended by the authors. We have had the greatest success with our clients using this approach.

The coordination of how the reengineering teams work together to best achieve their purpose is one of the functions of the steering team. The methodology and structure to be used may be clearly decided and agreed upon prior to the team chartering. If not done beforehand, it is a key stage in the chartering process whereby the steering team and the reengineering teams agree collectively on the most appropriate approach for the situation.

The Reengineering Team

Guidelines for Success

- The team is effectively chartered and has a clear understanding of its purpose.

- Boundaries are clearly defined and carefully managed.

- Team membership and leadership criteria are met.

- External customer involvement is utilized by the team.

- The team successfully works outside the paradigms set by the current process when redesigning the new process.

- The process effectively eliminates functional mindsets and works cross functionally.

- The team possesses a clear grasp of the elements of process design and is trained in both team dynamics and process design techniques and tools.

- Coordination of the work of the reengineering team to both the steering committee and to the other reengineering teams is carefully maintained and monitored.

- Functional and task conflicts are used constructively as sources of energy and creativity to generate team synergy.

Chartering the Team

Chartering Defined

Chartering is the process that establishes the "right" of the team to conduct its work as well as define the authority limits in which it can effectively accomplish its task. Teams that are not chartered effectively have a high rate of failure.

Chartering is the establishment of boundaries of empowerment within which a team (by mutual negotiation and agreement) can exercise the license to act freely.

Historically, a charter was a document that granted certain rights or defined the form of an institution. It established boundaries in terms of the rights and limitations that could be exercised by a group.

When teams are chartered, the chartering body must estimate the capability, willingness, and commitment of the team members to the reengineering effort. A leader's goal is to balance the team's ability with its desire for autonomy and independence and the need of completing the task in a timely and high quality manner. The challenge for the leader is to charter or empower the team at the outer limits of its capability boundaries.

Steps in the Chartering Process

1. State the issue - the problem, concern, area for improvement, or process.

2. Define the vision and the mission for the reengineering effort.

Chartering the Team

3. Set the critical success factors and their specific metrics.

4. Establish specific goals to be achieved and measures for assessing success.

5. Identify limitations - what are key limitations and boundaries of which the team should be aware?

6. Review and validate the team members - are these the most appropriate people to be placed on this team?

7. Identify the team sponsor and clarify the roles of the sponsor and the steering committee.

8. Determine level of authority - how much authority will be given to the team and for what decisions do they not have authority?

9. Confirm other requirements: schedule, budget, interim milestones.

10. Set the stage for creating the operating guidelines.

11. Create a conformance process - what is the mutually agreeable review process to be used at various points in the reengineering process?

Chartering the Team

Empowering the Team

Reengineering is an initiative that requires a team of committed, enthusiastic, knowledgeable people who recognize the need for change and are excited about making a collective contribution to this initiative. Accomplishing this requires effective empowerment of the reengineering team by the leadership in the organization. When the following criteria are met, an empowered team exists.

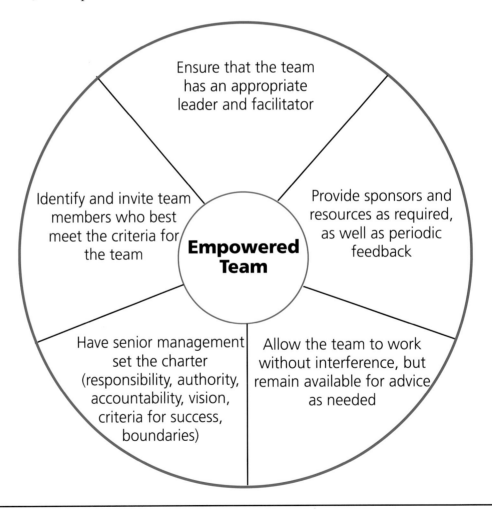

Critical Factors for Team Success

Introduction Characteristics of successful teams regardless of level or function are invariably consistent. The following general success factors apply to all teams. They are critical in ensuring overall synergy by the teams and the success of the reengineering effort through team effectiveness.

Organizational Factors
- A clearly defined and shared organizational vision
- Organizational learning gained collectively and reapplied among projects
- Clearly stated organizational priorities
- A high performance work environment that fosters teamwork
- Teamwork seen as a key factor in the organization's success

Management Factors
- Teams are sponsored and supported at senior management level
- Sponsorship actively demonstrated by senior managers
- Teams chartered at appropriate management levels with clearly defined boundaries and authority
- Senior management directly involved throughout the process
- Necessary resources made available
- Success, results and teamwork recognized and rewarded
- Team is chartered with a clearly defined purpose

Critical Factors for Team Success

Teamwork Factors

- Ongoing sponsorship and support

- Team's purpose is aligned with and perceived by its membership to contribute directly to organizational and/or project success

- Appropriate membership in terms of skill sets, disciplines and functions, and commitment

- Effective team leadership

- Clearly defined operating guidelines

- Effective team dynamics and interaction

- Defined problem-solving / process improvement model followed

- Appropriate amount of time allocated to meet and do the work

- Flexibility and creativity to overcome the barriers of business reality

- Clearly defined team accountability

Critical Factors for Team Success

Factors Contributing to Effective Teams

The following diagram depicts how organizational management behaviors, values, and the work environment play a vital role in fostering a culture for effective teamwork.

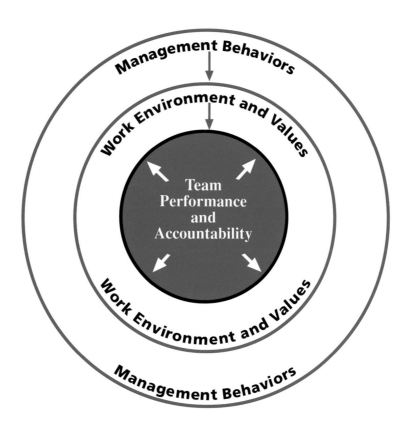

Critical Factors for Team Success

Characteristics of Effective Teams

Characteristic	Behaviors Demonstrated
Goal oriented	• Identifies and clarifies objectives • Commits to and accepts goals
Open minded	• Operates creatively • Free expression of ideas and suggestions
Result focused	• Stays on task • Produces required results
Process focused	• Clarifies roles and responsibilities • Identifies task and process behaviors
Organized	• Action plans are documented • Clear assignments made and accepted
Diverse	• Builds upon individual strengths • Respects functions and backgrounds
Leadership driven	• Leadership shifts based on skills • Supports organizational leadership
Team climate	• Informal, comfortable, relaxed atmosphere • No tensions or signs of boredom
Constructive disagreement	• Resolves conflict openly • Criticism without attack
Open communication	• All members participate in discussions • Active listening by everyone
Decisions through consensus	• Fact-based decision-making • Open evaluation and conflict resolution
Continuous improvement	• Evaluates its effectiveness • Improves its operating guidelines

Team Roles

More Than Just Team Members

A reengineering effort requires more than just a team of people assigned to complete the project. Many people and roles are vital in ensuring the success of the reengineering team. The following chart lists the main roles found within a reengineering effort, as well as their basic responsibilities.

Team Role	Purpose	Responsibilities
Team Leader	Directly guides the team through its work.	• Leads team efforts • Ensures team stays on task • Represents team to broader community
Team Facilitator	Helps generate team synergy through interpersonal and group processes.	• Guides team through consensus decision-making • Constructively deals with disagreement • Provides feedback regarding team performance
Team Members	Participate in the work of the team and support the achievement of its goals.	• Attend meetings and contribute fully • Accept and complete all assignments • Demonstrate commitment through participation and interpersonal behaviors
Organizational Leader (President or CEO)	Senior executive who leads organization through its reengineering efforts.	• Sets vision that motivates organization • Creates an environment that supports reengineering • Models commitment to the effort
Steering Team	Senior group that develops policies and strategies for reengineering.	• Determines priority of reengineering projects • Sets boundaries and charters the teams • Resolves conflicts among process owners • Endorses the final result
Team Sponsor	Provides managerial, organizational, political, and resource-related support.	• Informally monitors team progress • Ensures team has necessary resources • Represents team's interest to senior management

Team Roles

Team Role	Purpose	Responsibilities
Trainer	Provides formal training for reengineering throughout the organization.	• Provides necessary instruction to teams • Provides materials to meet needs
Coach	Provides support to teams in technical, process, or interpersonal issues.	• Assists teams with problems that hamper progress • Listens and offers advice or suggestions • Provides coaching and counseling to team leader as requested
Process Owner	Person responsible for a specific process.	• Provides data regarding current process characteristics and performance • Assists and provides input to the team as needed • Participates in the endorsement process • Responsible for implementing the reengineered process after endorsement

Team Leader

Every reengineering team requires a team leader whose primary role is to ensure that the team achieves its goals.

Criteria for Selecting Team Leaders

- Knowledgeable regarding process
- Objective
- Good listener
- Has good management network
- Encourages participation
- Delegates effectively
- Encourages cooperation and trust
- Is respected by others

Team Roles

**Team
Facilitator**

Every reengineering team should also have a team facilitator whose primary role is to ensure that the team maintains a positive and productive work climate and effective team processes.

Criteria for Selecting Team Facilitators

- Encourages participation and cooperation
- Provides assistance to others
- Manages conflict constructively
- Addresses/resolves disruptive behavior
- Assists people in expressing ideas
- Helps team members feel included
- Solicits and administers feedback

**Team
Members**

Reengineering is an initiative that requires a team of committed, enthusiastic, knowledgeable individuals who recognize the need for change and are excited about making a collective contribution to this initiative. The team is usually drawn from the individuals who work closely with the process being addressed. They can be from different work areas, and have a variety of skills and knowledge.

Criteria for Selecting Team Members

- Willing to listen, contribute, invest time and energy
- Open and flexible to new ideas
- Knowledgeable regarding the process
- Focused on team goal instead of personal agenda

Operating Guidelines

Team Operating Guidelines Overview

The rules defining governance and behavior that a team develops for itself are often called "operating guidelines." These guidelines determine how the team will function. As a team, members should answer the following questions for themselves.

1. How will goals and objectives be established?

2. How will we assign and accept roles and tasks?

3. How will we solve problems and share information?

4. How will we make decisions?

5. How will we deal with changes?

6. How will we resolve issues and manage conflict?

7. How will we interface with all the other stakeholders in the process?

8. How will we monitor or change things that are not producing results?

9. How will we evaluate the effectiveness of our work and our performance as a team?

These are some of the questions that help shape the team's operating guidelines.

Operating Guidelines

Below is a graphic depicting a typical process or sequence for ongoing team operations and performance.

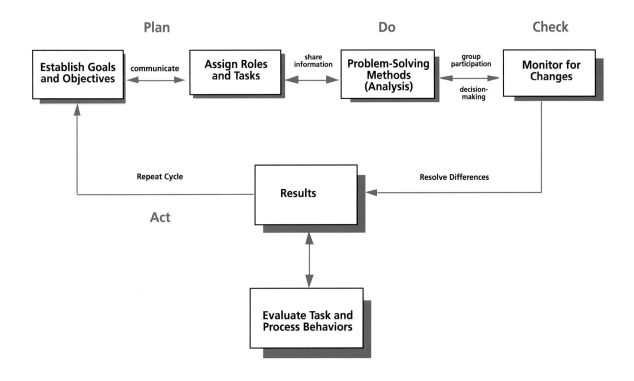

Operating Guidelines

Consensus Decision Making

One guideline that must be determined is how the team will make decisions. Consensus is the most appropriate method for decision making in a reengineering context. Consensus is the process by which a team comes to a decision - an agreement - to which all members of the team are willing to make a commitment and provide support. Not all members may have made this decision as their personal choice. However, each member sees sufficient merit in the decision to make the commitment to support it.

Consensus is not:

- Compromise
- Voting
- Abdication
- Deference to authority
- Unanimity

Consensus is agreement through discussion based on a genuine willingness to understand all the points of view regarding a situation.

Guidelines for Consensus Decision Making

In order to effectively implement the process of achieving consensus, team members must be able to put their own personal agendas aside and consider what is best for the team and its goals. Disagreement should be viewed as helping the team make the best decision. True consensus is reached when everyone feels that their ideas are valued and respected, and the final team decision merits everyone's support.

Operating Guidelines

Below are some general guidelines for generating consensus.

- Generate appropriate information
- Seek different opinions from everybody
- Present your opinion logically and clearly
- Listen to reactions of others
- Do not argue from a fixed position
- Remain open to new possibilities and alternatives
- Involve all in the process
- Encourage disagreements focused on "what's right," not on "who's right"
- Do not change your mind just to avoid conflict
- Do not use majority vote
- Promote win/win
- Look for the best alternative

Guidelines for Team Meetings

One of the most difficult things that teams can do is run effective meetings that generate positive results and leave everyone feeling that something has been accomplished. There are five purposes for team meetings.

1. *Define the team:* Some meetings establish who the team members will be and clarify their roles. These initial meetings help build understanding and commitment and generate enthusiasm to the team effort.

Operating Guidelines

2. *Share information:* A meeting is an efficient way of ensuring that everyone is operating with the same information. Questions can be answered and clarified to provide a common baseline of knowledge and agreement.

3. *Generate ideas and make decisions:* Meetings provide a forum for team discussion that can generate synergy. Synergistic outcomes are highly supported by the team, and usually contain the best solutions.

4. *Assign responsibility and manage implementation:* Meetings provide a good opportunity for allocating responsibilities and tasks based on the resources and expertise of the team.

5. *Review progress:* Meetings are an effective tool for assessing progress on a team task and initiating modifications if the team is not meeting its goals.

Team Meeting Guidelines

- Hold enough meetings to keep members informed and committed
- Promptly publish minutes which reflect accomplishments and agendas
- Maintain good communication between meetings
- Enforce attention to standards
- Prepare meeting agendas with specific objectives
- Each meeting should have a leader, facilitator, and recorder
- The leader should drive toward action
- The leader or facilitator should help the team gain consensus and commit to its decisions
- The team recorder should document key issues, decisions, and follow up action items

Conclusion

The role of teams is becoming increasingly important for organizations in general. It is important to recognize, however, that teams are not the best solution for all decisions or for the implementation of all work. They are the best vehicle when the interdependence among team members is high; commitment to the solution is required among all the team members; there is no obvious expert; or a synergistic result is required. Teams should be used to solve organizational problems when one or more of these criteria are present.

Because reengineering meets all four of these key criteria, teams and teamwork are essential to the success of business process reengineering.

Chapter Four

The Reengineering Process and Tools

Components of Reengineering

Introduction

There are two types of reengineering: reengineering a business process (simple or complex), and reengineering an organization (in whole or in part). Reengineering an entire organization - or a department or function within that organization - is significantly different from reengineering a process or system. Organizational reengineering requires a broader inquiry and a set of solutions that are much broader in scope than process reengineering. The focus of this book is business process reengineering and the model that follows in this chapter is geared toward business process reengineering only.

Business Process Reengineering

Many processes are improved through the application of continuous process improvement techniques. While valuable, this inherent methodology is based on process stabilization followed by incremental improvement. Many sub-processes to core business processes may be significantly improved using this methodology. However, these improvements are not focused on radically changing the components, basic relationships, and output of an organization's core business processes.

This is not to imply that significant improvements in customer satisfaction or cost reduction are not forthcoming from continuous improvement or total quality initiatives. However, they are not designed to challenge the core purpose or assumptions underlying a business process. For this reason, the incremental improvements gained by a continuous improvement process typically do not deliver the breakthrough results many organizations require in order to position themselves for a competitive advantage in a time frame consistent with their business needs and goals.

Components of Reengineering

Business Process Reengineering

Many organizations have concluded that the type of transformation required to provide the significant results sought needs a fundamentally different approach to how the organization produces and delivers its core products and services.

Business Process Reengineering (or redesign) - if effectively sponsored, planned and implemented - can provide dramatic results, measured by increased customer satisfaction, reduced costs of service delivery or production, improved performance, enhanced return on investments and improved organizational dynamics.

Reengineering is not for the faint-hearted. It requires a willingness to undergo critical self-analysis, to encounter change of the broadest and deepest kind, and to maintain the discipline required of a rigorous process. When approached with commitment, it can serve as a tool that fundamentally and permanently alters the competitive position of an organization, enabling it to meet the challenges it will face in the months and years ahead.

Components of Reengineering

Requirements

- A leadership commitment of time, resources and behavior that enables and sustains transformational change.

- Permission for the organization or process to be redesigned in its entirety. This includes some non-traditional approaches to the way in which information and data are shared.

- Radical and creative change in the approach to how the organization or core business process delivers its output.

- Redesign from a functionally-driven hierarchy to cross-functional lines of responsibilities in which process ownership becomes the measure of accountability for results.

- A clear charter (goals and expectations) for the team(s) formed to lead the reengineering process.

- Goals that are multifaceted: customer satisfaction, performance, cost, cycle time, flexibility, and speed. The results must be significantly more substantial than those that can be generated through other traditional improvement methods.

The Reengineering Roadmap: Defining the Process

Structure

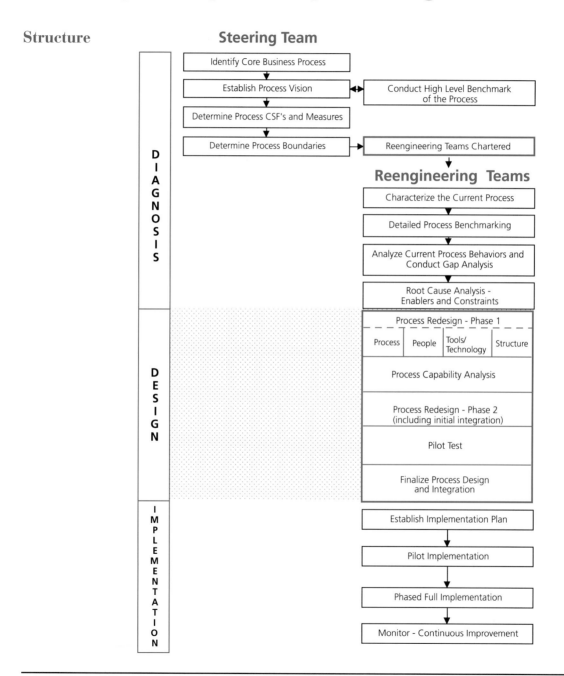

Steering Team

| Identify Core Business Process |
| Establish Process Vision | → | Conduct High Level Benchmark of the Process |
| Determine Process CSF's and Measures |
| Determine Process Boundaries | Reengineering Teams Chartered |

DIAGNOSIS

Reengineering Teams

- Characterize the Current Process
- Detailed Process Benchmarking
- Analyze Current Process Behaviors and Conduct Gap Analysis
- Root Cause Analysis - Enablers and Constraints

DESIGN

Process Redesign - Phase 1

| Process | People | Tools/Technology | Structure |

Process Capability Analysis

Process Redesign - Phase 2 (including initial integration)

Pilot Test

Finalize Process Design and Integration

IMPLEMENTATION

- Establish Implementation Plan
- Pilot Implementation
- Phased Full Implementation
- Monitor - Continuous Improvement

The Reengineering Roadmap: Defining the Process

Reengineering can only be successfully achieved when it is an initiative supported fully by the senior management of the organization and designed by the people using the current process who will be responsible for implementing the new process. This diverse team of people now faces the challenge of conducting the reengineering endeavor. This endeavor will take them through the steps in the model shown on the previous page, which will be the focus of this section: reviewing the steps and procedures of implementing a structured reengineering process. The structure of business process reengineering moves through three major phases of development, as shown in the previous diagram and described below.

Diagnosis

This diagnosis phase involves the steering team and the initial stages of the reengineering team. In this phase the desired vision for the process is established; the process is benchmarked to establish and validate potential capability; and the current process is analyzed to define current operating conditions as well as constraints to operations.

Design

In this next phase the new process is designed. The design includes the flowcharting of the process itself; people aspects of the new process; tools required; and the technological and structural requirements. The design stage is conducted in phases, with pilot testing to ensure its ability to meet the critical success factors and vision.

The Reengineering Roadmap: Defining the Process

Implementation

The third phase is also conducted in stages. The first stage takes the pilot developed in the design phase and converts it into steady state use. The remaining elements are then staged into full implementation with constant measuring to ensure performance. Once installed and fully operational, the new process is ready for the ongoing continuous improvement process that should be inherent in all business processes.

The next several pages are mapped to the diagram for process reengineering and provide a capsule overview of the activities and results contained within each step of the process.

Diagnosis

> ### Identify Core Business Process

In this step the steering team - which is typically the senior management of the organization - identifies the core business processes driving the organization. Typically, an organization has five to eight such processes. If analyzed using a tree diagramming process, these core processes serve as the basis for governing the entire business. This can guide the shift from a functional, hierarchical orientation to a customer-driven, cross-functional, process-centered approach for managing and continuously improving the organization. Once the business processes have been identified, they are prioritized by this team for reengineering based on a combination of need and opportunity.

The Reengineering Roadmap: Defining the Process

Establish the Process Vision

Just as the organization has a vision, so should a vision be crafted for the core business process to be reengineered. This vision should capture the imagination of the reengineering team to reach beyond incremental improvements and create a process that generates a sustained competitive advantage for the organization.

High Level Benchmark of the Process

The steering team must conduct a high level external benchmark analysis of the process as a step in setting its vision. Unless there is some knowledge of the results current industry leaders are achieving regarding this process, the vision may be set too low and not create competitive advantage, or may be set unrealistically high and be unachievable. As with all benchmarking, the review should not be limited to the industry in which the company is akin, but extended to any environment in which this or a similar process is deployed.

Determine Process CSFs and Measures

The Critical Success Factors for the process define what must be accomplished for it to be successful for the organization. CSFs may address issues of technical performance. They may also include issues such as marketplace focus; customer satisfaction; cycle time; cost implications; degrees of accuracy and technical quality; technological sophistication, etc. For each CSF the measure or measures must be identified in order to

The Reengineering Roadmap: Defining the Process

Diagnosis

determine whether the CSF is being achieved. Measures are defined in categories of quantity, quality, time, or budget.

Determine Process Boundaries

Every process has boundaries beyond which it cannot or should not extend. Boundary conditions are essential because they help guide the chartering of the reengineering team. Boundary conditions may include the start and stop points of the core business process. They may also describe business products or services to be included or excluded for the process. Similar boundaries may be set for markets or customers. Boundary conditions may also be established for areas of cost, physical space, technology, equipment, personnel, or other internal limitations and requirements.

Chartering the Reengineering Team

This step is described in greater detail in other sections of this book. The chartering process is essential because it signals the formal transfer of ownership of the reengineering initiative from the steering team to the reengineering team. In this step all goals, boundary conditions and requirements are fully defined. Proper chartering is one of the most crucial steps of the entire reengineering process.

The Reengineering Roadmap: Defining the Process

Characterize the Current Process

The characterization of the current process is the first step conducted by the reengineering team. This step is designed to help the team fully understand the current process prior to designing a new process. The process is flowcharted and the flowchart is validated by users. Users and owners are identified as well as interim and final customers of the process. Inputs and outputs are identified for all key steps of the current process. Finally, the current input, formative and output measures for the process are identified.

Detailed Process Benchmarking

This process must now be subjected to detailed internal and external benchmarking. In the internal benchmarking step, any comparable internal processes should be analyzed to assess their performance. In addition, the measures of performance of the current process must be gathered, showing both the upper and lower ranges of performance, as well as the general performance levels with standard deviations and any other formal measures available. Benchmarking may include feedback from internal and external customer groups as well.

The external benchmarking process is a detailed and thorough investigation of other organizations to identify best practices. Suppliers and customers are good sources of information regarding possible benchmark processes. The benchmarking must be detailed. It is essential that not only is the

The Reengineering Roadmap: Defining the Process

Diagnosis

result of the benchmark process known, but how benchmark firms achieve their results. Understanding how results are achieved may impact the redesign process, or may define processes that are not possible for your organization due to defined constraints or boundary conditions.

Analyze Process Behaviors and Conduct Gap Analysis

In this step the desired behaviors of the process are identified. That is, if this process were meeting its vision and critical success factors, what would it look like in terms of both implementation and outputs? Behaviors should be identified for each critical success factor. Once identified, the current behaviors of the current process should now be reviewed. The difference between current and ideal performance is the gap analysis. This will define the key areas where work will need to be focused in the new process design stage.

Root Cause Analysis - Identify Enablers and Constraints

The next step is to determine why the current process fails to meet the desired vision and critical success factors. This root cause analysis will once again help define the design process. As part of this analysis, constraints to the current process are identified. Removal of these constraints may be key to the successful redesign effort. Enablers should also be identified. If possible, enablers should be maintained and strengthened in the process redesign to support successful implementation.

The Reengineering Roadmap: Defining the Process

Design

Process Redesign - Phase 1

In Phase 1 of the redesign effort, the first version of the newly reengineered process is crafted. This redesign should contain four elements: process, people, tools and structure. The process element creates a new flow of how the process should actually work to meet its critical success factors, achieve the measures required, and fulfill the process vision. People considerations include the number of resources required, roles, individual or team efforts, training requirements, implications for recognition and reward systems, etc. Tools include all the physical, technological, paper-based, etc. requirements that will be needed to support the process. Structure examines the organizational structure to determine whether there are any constraints to the implementation of this cross-functional process. Structural change recommendations are included as part of this total redesign. Technological requirements (such as information processing) are identified at this time.

Process Capability Analysis

After the new process has been initially crafted, it must be analyzed to determine whether it has the capability to meet its requirements if installed as proposed. Furthermore, a separate analysis must be performed to determine whether the organization has the capability to install the proposed process. This analysis is accomplished with both external benchmarking and internal focus group feedback. Based on feedback regarding these two factors, adjustments to the process can now be made.

The Reengineering Roadmap: Defining the Process

Design

Process Redesign - Phase 2

In this phase, all the feedback from the capability analysis is integrated and the process is redesigned to address all capability issues. The process is now "alpha tested" and deployed in test conditions to see whether it meets performance expectations. This phase is not complete until the process can meet its requirements under these designated test conditions.

Pilot Test New Process Design

The process is now subjected to a pilot or "beta test." Under these conditions, a small section of the organization uses the process as intended under live conditions. This pilot test is used to determine process capability; identify flaws in design; assess robustness under use; and identify any other needed changes.

Finalize Process Design

All concerns identified in the pilot test are now analyzed to modify the process and create the final integration of the new process. This integrated process is now ready to be subjected to formal endorsement by user groups, the process owner, suppliers and customers of the process, and the steering team. Once endorsed, the stage has been set for implementation.

The Reengineering Roadmap: Defining the Process

Implementation
| **Establish Implementation Plan** |

A plan for a phased implementation should now be crafted. The plan must address issues regarding the development of tools required; structural adjustments to be made; training of personnel as needed; and communication of the new process to all stakeholders. The plan should also define what will be done, when, by whom, and how. Budgetary or other constraints are addressed at this time as well. Prior to implementation, this plan must be approved by both the process owner and the steering team.

| **Pilot Implementation** |

Core business processes must not be treated lightly. Presuming that a switch can be turned and a core process can be replaced without disruption to ongoing business operations is both naive and foolhardy. For this reason, a pilot implementation should first be installed. The scope and length of the pilot will be determined by circumstances. The pilot should not be considered finished until the process in the pilot has stabilized and is consistently meeting the vision, critical success factors and measures required. If the pilot cannot be stabilized at this level, it should be returned for redesign rather than implementation being continued.

The Reengineering Roadmap: Defining the Process

Implementation

Phased Full Implementation

Once the pilot is stabilized, implementation can proceed. If possible, implementation should be conducted in phases. Phases may involve groups of customers; groups of products; geographic areas; parts of a plant; etc. Installing the new process in stages increases the probability of success, is least disruptive to ongoing operations, and creates the highest level of commitment and support throughout the organization.

Monitor - Continuous Improvement

Once fully installed and stabilized, the process should now be monitored regularly as an ongoing part of normal business operations. This will ensure that its steady state condition meets or exceeds all critical success factor requirements. As soon as the process meets these requirements, it should become an integral part of the organization's continuous improvement process and regularly be reviewed for constant and continuous improvement.

Team Tools

The Purpose of Team Tools

Every organization that embraces a reengineering effort requires employees who can work in teams to detect problem areas, analyze the results to identify the issues, and create effective solutions that can be implemented. In order to achieve this, reengineering teams need to be skilled in the tools for problem solving and analysis as well as in the creation of solutions and process design. These tools include methods, sometimes mathematical, that collect and measure data to help the team analyze and create solutions.

The following pages provide suggestions to help teams decide which tools are appropriate in their work. Then, each category of tools is broken out further. These tools are the common ones which have been found to be effective in reengineering efforts. Each tool has value at different points in the reengineering process.

When to Use Tools

There are generally three situations that face process reengineering teams:

- Generating ideas and gathering information
- Analyzing data
- Creating solutions

There are a number of tools that teams can use in each of these three stages.

Team Tools

Generating Ideas and Gathering Information

Reengineering teams typically face situations where they need to gather information about the process. They may need to generate new thoughts about the way the current process is working or gather information regarding the process flow. The flowchart, for example, ensures everyone on the team fully understands the current process that is under review. Very often, these situations occur when a team deals with a process that has never been studied in detail. The team members also may not agree on the best way to deal with the process or the most appropriate next steps. It is then vital to gather as much information as possible about the way the current process works and generate everyone's ideas so all team members are approaching the process from the same base of knowledge. The following pages give examples of the most useful tools for this purpose and the results offered to the team.

Some of the tools for generating ideas use brainstorming as the source of ideas. The affinity diagram, nominal group technique and the cause and effect diagram, sometimes called fishbone diagram, provide a structure to help teams order the results of brainstorming. The easiest way to gather data is often to ask people who use the process. A survey, focus group or interview will help gather facts, data and opinions about the process and allow the teams to evaluate the information. These tools help the team identify the gap between how the process is working and user expectations.

Team Tools

Checksheet Diagram

Purpose: To determine the frequency of certain events in the process.

Result: Identify typical problems/results and their relative frequencies.

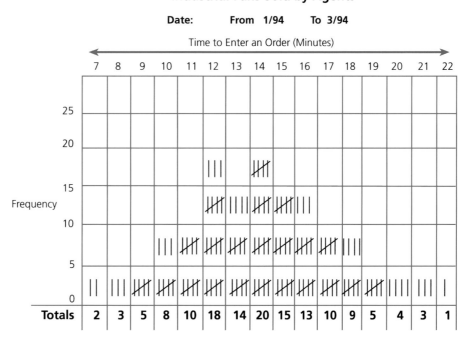

Industrial Fans Sold by Agents

Date: From 1/94   To 3/94

Time to Enter an Order (Minutes)

	7	8	9	10	11	12	13	14	15	16	17	18	19	20	21	22
Totals	2	3	5	8	10	18	14	20	15	13	10	9	5	4	3	1

This example is a process distribution checksheet. It is easy to create and captures the information for the team in an immediately useful form. Checksheets are simple to use and very effective.

Team Tools

Force Field Analysis

Purpose: To identify and reduce anticipated resistance to change.

Result: Facilitates movement toward change.

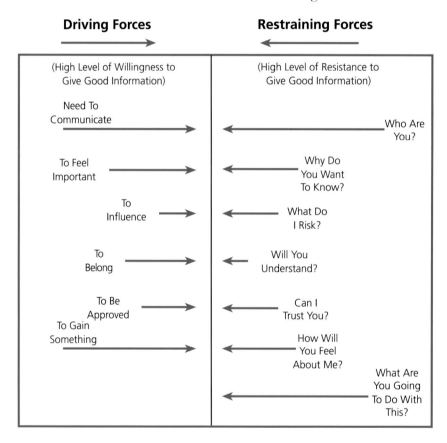

A force field analysis assists the team in appreciating the impact of a change to a process in an organization.

Team Tools

Affinity Diagram

Purpose: To gather large numbers of ideas and categorize them into groups.

Result: Brings idea generation process to its next level of sophistication.

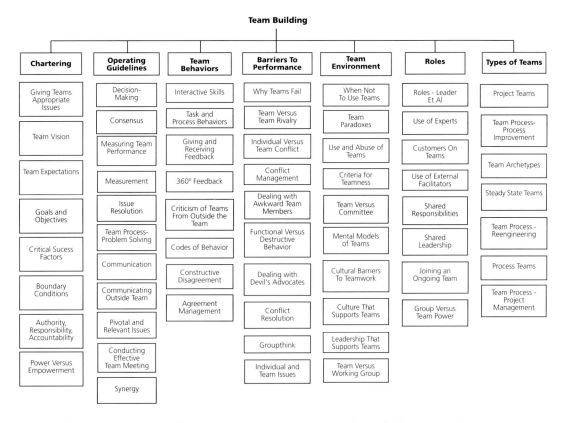

The affinity diagram allows the teams to group ideas following a brainstorming session into natural groupings in a simple but very effective manner. The title boxes are added once the team is satisfied with the outcome.

Team Tools

Customer Requirements Analysis

Purpose: To determine what customers need and expect from the process output.

Result: Creates clarity regarding what customers require of this process.

	Dimensions	Questions	Customer Requirements	Current Status
Description	Description	What is the product, service or information?		
	Outcomes / Effects	What results does it produce?		
	Use	How is it used, and by whom?		
	Format	How should it be organized, presented, packaged, laid out?		
	Location	Where is it needed and used?		
	Context	Are there legal, policy, procedural, environmental, safety requirements?		
	Additional Factors	What additional factors (environmental, personal, interpersonal) are important?		
Measures	Quantitative Standards	How many? How much?		
	Qualitative Standards	Issues related to ease of utilization.		
	Time	When is it needed and used, and for how long?		
	Costs / Benefits	How much does this cost? What are the benefits derived?		

This is a generic set of questions which enable the team to create a series of questions for an interview series, focus groups or survey instrument.

Team Tools

Flowchart Process Measures

Purpose: To identify how a process currently works and identify measuring points.

Result: Give insight into the interactions among work steps that lead to better solutions and current performance.

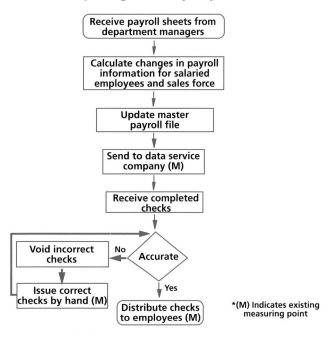

Preparing Monthly Payroll

The flowchart enables the whole team to clearly understand the process under review. Often this is the first time everyone on the team sees how it works which allows for discussion.

Team Tools

Analyzing Data

Reengineering teams must analyze the data and information they collect to determine the most likely causes of the problems with the process and to choose the best solutions for implementation. Careful analysis of the data will show a team the precise trouble points and very often shows them the path to the solution. The components of a solution tend to come out of a proper analysis of the data and information collected by the reengineering team. The following pages show the most commonly used tools for this purpose and their benefits to the team.

In particular, concepts such as the pareto principle and prioritization matrices assist teams to focus on where to place the available resources to provide the greatest impact in the shortest possible time or, at least, cost.

Creating Solutions

Once data have been collected and analyzed, the reengineering team must decide on the most appropriate solutions to the process. This can at first appear to be an overwhelming task. Various team members may have different opinions about which solutions to implement and what is the most important area to tackle. Reengineering teams quite often use tools to help them determine the best solution for the given process. This section outlines three tools that help the reengineering team focus its efforts on the most appropriate solution for the process.

Team Tools

Cause and Effect Diagram

Purpose: To identify and categorize various possible causes of a problem.

Result: Serves as a guide for discussion and focuses team meetings.

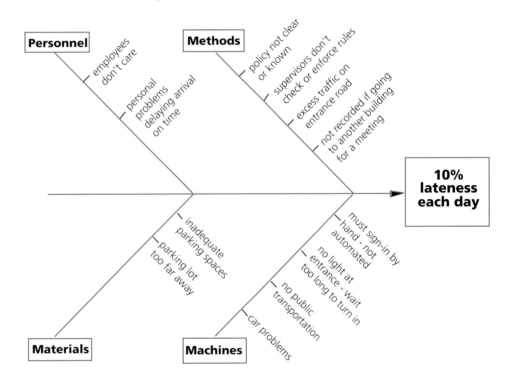

This example shows the (many) causes of the single effect, 10% lateness each day, observed by a team. Each spine has its own title and forms a subject for the team to consider in relationship to the effect.

Team Tools

Run Chart

Purpose: To track processes in which data needs to be assessed regularly.

Result: Show the quantitative outputs of a process over time.

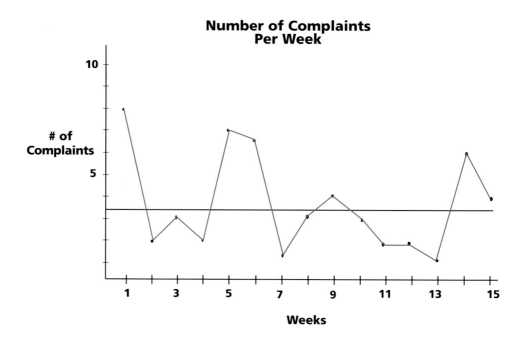

The challenge for the team is clear. What causes the complaints to move above the mean about once a month? Is it a problem with the month end pressure to ship by deadlines? The team now has a starting point for further analysis.

Team Tools

Gap Analysis

Purpose: To define the "gap" between current and desired performance.

Result: Identifies key areas that need a reengineering effort.

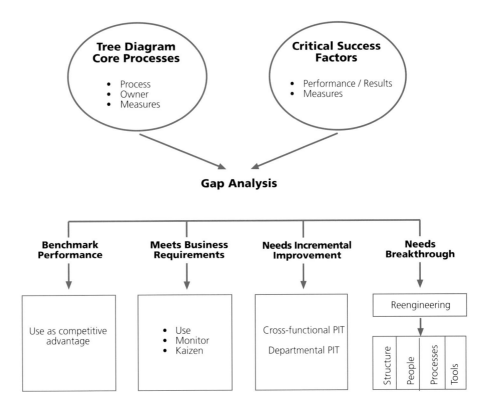

Careful study by a team can provide a clear decision path that will set priorities for the processes that need more urgent attention and will render the most benefit to the company.

Team Tools

Pareto Chart

Purpose: To show the degree of influence of each variable on a particular event.

Result: Identify critical variables that create numerous problems.

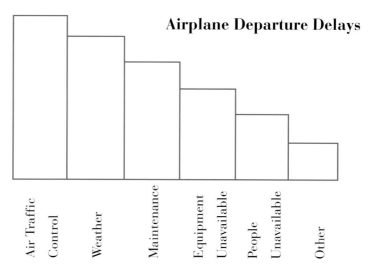

Airplane Departure Delays

The use and interpretation of Pareto Charts is based on a concept referred to as the Pareto Principle. This principle was developed by an Italian economist, Vilfredo Pareto, who at the time discovered that 20% of his country's population owned 80% of the wealth. This discovery led to the concept that in many situations, 20% of the problems caused 80% of the result. Using this concept, teams can focus on the "vital few" problems as opposed to the "trivial many." The Pareto Chart is helpful in identifying the biggest problems on which a team may focus to provide the relative importance of information.

Team Tools

Prioritization Matrix

Purpose: To measure solutions against important criteria.

Result: Ensures decision making based on priority, not preference.

Serial #	Variable	Criteria						Perf. Index	Count
		A weighting factor can be used to provide more sophistication.							

This matrix is valuable to the team and enables it to order priorities and come to consensus on the best or most important activity or component of a solution.

Team Tools

Tree Diagram

Purpose: To identify all factors or elements involved in solution implementation.

Result: Defines all issues and tasks to complete during implementation.

The tree diagram breaks down a major task into the constituent parts that must be undertaken to complete the task. As the chart moves from left to right the level of specificity increases to a point where the team can assign people to specific tasks.

Team Tools

Gantt Chart

Purpose: To identify the overall scope of the implementation of a solution.

Result: Helps the team analyze the tasks and time frame of a solution.

	Key Actions/ Tasks	Responsibility	Week of: 1	2	3	4	5	6	7	8	9	10	11	12	13	14	15
Solution Component																	
Solution Component																	
Solution Component																	

This classic planning tool is useful to a team to set a time schedule for the completed reengineering process.

Transition to Operations

Involving the Rest of the Organization

Once the reengineering team has a recommended solution for the identified process, it must determine how to involve the rest of the organization to ensure a smooth transition from design to operations. There are four key factors involved in making this transition successful. The first is to establish a good communications strategy. The reengineering team must consistently inform management of its progress. This helps to ensure that the team is moving on the right track. The second factor is implementation planning. The reengineering team must think carefully about the best way to implement its solutions and create a plan that considers all perspectives. The third factor is the presentation. The reengineering team must present its solution to the steering team for endorsement. This presentation can be a positive tool in gaining commitment to the proposed solution. The final factor is the implementation itself, enabling all employees to be involved and, therefore, committed to the success of the new business process.

Communication Strategy

The bridge between the reengineering team and management is a vital factor in the success of the reengineering effort. Reengineering team members must always feel that these lines of communication are open and that management supports their efforts. Management serves as a crucial sounding board for the reengineering team. They guide the process and help air difficult issues that may hinder team progress. This communication also allows management to be more involved with the process of reengineering and, therefore, more committed to the solutions of the team. The strategy is to ensure that these lines of communication exist before the reengineering team begins its work and that the reengineering team is clear about what results management expects. In this manner, when the team

Transition to Operations

makes its final presentation it can be sure that it is on the right track with its solution. The steering team should serve as the sponsor and bridge builder to ensure effective ongoing communications and support from management and the process owner.

Implementation Planning

Developing a comprehensive implementation plan takes the "what" of the proposed solution and turns it into the "how."

Tasks of implementation: The tasks describe the "what" that is to occur. These can be taken from the previously created tree diagrams or gantt charts.

Context of implementation: The context describes the "how" of the plan, including a comprehensive description of how the implementation will be supported by management.

Factors that can foster or hinder implementation: These factors detail the aids and barriers facing the implementation process. They consider resistance at all levels of the organization, as well as potential resources that can assist in the implementation process. A force field analysis can be a useful tool in identifying the factors for and against the plan.

Transition to Operations

**The
Presentation**

The following key points illustrate the best way to ensure the successful presentation of the proposed implementation plan:

- Involve all members of the reengineering team in both the design and the presentation

- Make the presentation to those who can make the final decision (the steering team)

- Use visuals and keep the presentation short and to the point

- Be prepared to answer questions and issues raised by management

- The presentation is not the forum to push for a decision

**Organization
Implementation**

After the solution has been approved, the team should begin implementation throughout the organization. An implementation team should be formed which may require a shift in membership from the reengineering team. The implementation team should involve key individuals and functions whose roles will change due to this implementation. It is essential to select an implementation leader who has the full responsibility, authority and accountability for the implementation of the plan. Adjustments will, of course, need to be made at various points in the implementation process. The team and management should recognize that adjustments are a natural result of any implementation. A re-chartering exercise may be very useful for this implementation team.

Transition to Operations

Monitor the New Process

Monitoring the new process serves two purposes. The first is to ensure that the improvements have become part of the steady state operations of the organization. The second purpose is to ensure that the improvements are long-term and sustaining and not simply the consequence of increased attention being given to this process for a short period of time (the Hawthorne effect).

The implementation team must formally complete its work and management must have received and acknowledged the benefits of the work of these teams. This enables the team to formally disband. This final step should be implemented after sufficient monitoring of the process has been performed so that the results of the team have been achieved as the new steady state condition of the organization.

Chapter Five

Measuring Results

What to Measure

Importance of Measures

It is the engineer's axiom that "You don't really understand something until you can measure it." Although this statement may not be literally true all the time, it is a good perspective to use when designing and implementing business processes. Without measurement of business processes there is no way to know whether a process is creating the desired results; whether the results are consistent and within the defined boundaries; or whether the performance of a process is stable, improving or deteriorating. Measurement, therefore, is a fundamental component of both developing and using business processes.

The Basis for Measurement

What is the basis against which measurement criteria and processes should be established? The answer has been developed throughout the re-engineering process. Measurements are based upon customer requirements and the critical success factors for the process. The customer requirements should have been carefully diagnosed and embedded into the critical success factors. This is a good time to validate that they indeed are addressed fully through the CSFs. In the process of defining the CSFs, one or several measures were identified for each. These form the basis for the output measures of the process and the basis on which the measurement system is installed.

There are three categories for which measurements should be created: process inputs; process throughputs; and process outputs.

What to Measure

**Process
Inputs**

Process inputs represent the data and information that come from outside the process and are required to create value. A large percentage of the input typically comes at the beginning of the process. For example, if this is an order fulfillment process, the primary input may be a form submitted by the sales organization from which orders can be processed. If this is an engineering design process, the initial inputs may be a set of specifications sent by the customer or an internal data base from which design criteria and components can be drawn.

Process inputs do not come solely at the beginning of the process. They may enter when information is needed for the process to continue. In the case of the order fulfillment process, data may be required regarding current manufacturing capacities and schedules to know when the new order can be integrated into the manufacturing schedule. In the case of the engineering design process, customer feedback or new information from vendors may enter at various points along the process.

Many inputs can be planned and controlled throughout the process. Other process inputs may come at any time. Change orders from customers, for example, may come unexpectedly. The process must have a way of integrating unexpected inputs.

All key inputs should be identified and measurement systems installed to monitor these inputs. One of the purposes of measurements is to monitor the quantity of these inputs. Another may be to assess their timeliness. A third criterion may be to gauge the quality of the inputs.

What to Measure

For example, a process may not be meeting its output criteria and may be thought to be flawed. On examination, however, it may be the quality or timeliness of the inputs that are the issue and the solution is in a different inputting process.

The ability to measure inputs is critical to assessing whether the process meets its throughput requirements and achieves the required results.

Process Throughputs

Once the process has its inputs - at whatever place they may appear - it initiates the steps by which it creates its value. If there is no measurement between input and output, however, the process becomes a "black box." No one can really know what is going on inside. Then, when the process fails to perform, it is very difficult to correct it. For this reason, it is essential to identify key measures along the way as individual transactions move through the process. This is known as throughput.

Throughputs do not necessarily have to be identified at every step of the process. Some steps are so short or so inextricably tied to other steps that it would be redundant, time consuming and unnecessarily costly to measure every step. There are two key places where throughput measures are essential. Process throughput should be measured at those steps where a key output is created or a key value added. These are the points at which the transaction should not proceed if it is not correct. Every such point must be measured as an integral part of the process. This is precisely how quality gets built into the process rather than being "added on" later through a separate inspection system.

What to Measure

Process Throughputs

The second place where throughput measures should be installed is at key points of interface or hand-off. This is especially true at points where the process may cross functional boundaries. At these points it is essential to know that the output of one step and the required input for the next step are identical and that the hand-off is continuous and seamless.

Process Outputs

The final measures for the process are its output: the end result of the process. Output measures must correspond to what the customers of the process require and the inputs of the next step to which this process flows. If the process yields a result that is transmitted directly to the customer, then the process must meet all customer requirements. Process outputs must also be measured against the process critical success factors.

There is one other criterion that should be applied to process output measures. They must be cumulative over time and reportable to show the ongoing performance of the process. Since this is a core business process, its output is essential to the success of the business. The process output data should be an integral part of the management information system that is reported regularly (typically monthly) to review the overall performance of the business. Key process output measures must be drafted in such a manner that they can be "rolled up," synthesized, compared to other windows of time, and integrated with other critical measures of the firm. When implemented properly, process output measures are a natural result of the process itself and make reporting activities of the firm simple, straightforward, and a seamless part of ongoing operations.

What to Measure

The diagram below shows the relationship of input, throughput, and output data to each other.

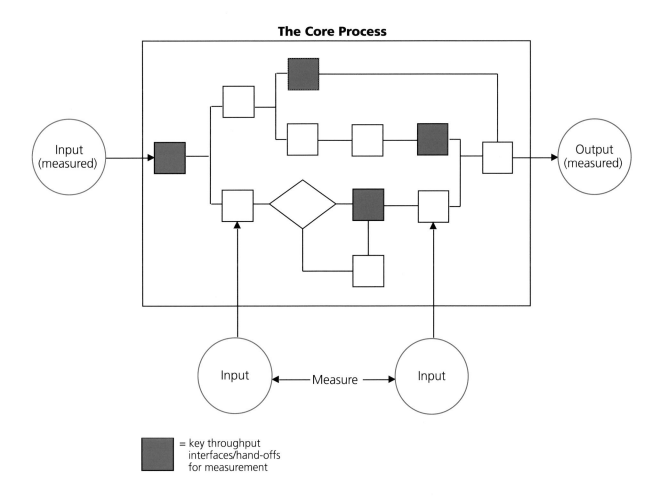

What to Measure

Types of Data

There are many ways to categorize and describe the data that are used in all stages of measurement. It is useful at this point to make the distinction between variable and attribute data. Variable data can be gathered along a continuum. Measures such as number of errors per item; temperature; weight; percentage accuracy; and cost per unit can be placed on a continuum, plotted and analyzed through a variety of statistical means. Such tools as averages, standard deviations, histograms, and correlative and causal studies are applied to variable data.

On the other hand, there are some types of data that cannot be measured against a variable scale but are nonetheless quite important. These units of data can only be placed into categories. This type of data is known as attribute data: categories or groups that share common attributes. How many people in a group have brown eyes, blue eyes or other colors is a good example of attribute data. How many products were produced of each color? Checklists are one of the most common tools used to collect attribute data.

Some data can be gathered in both ways. For example, the weight of individuals can be taken as a variable number, averaged, shown in standard deviations, and placed on a scale. On the other hand, people could be classified as underweight, within acceptable boundaries or overweight. In this case, the data would be treated as attribute.

Variable data is more precise, but often more difficult to gather. On the other hand, attribute data can be treated like variable data and reveal numbers that really don't have much meaning.

What to Measure

Neither form of data is inherently preferable; the type should be related to the information needed for high quality analysis and decision-making. Just as Frank Lloyd Wright said about his buildings: "Form should follow function."

Measurement Criteria

The last question in the "what to measure" category speaks to the different criteria against which data can be measured. Many teams have found it quite useful to think about this question in terms of four categories: quantity, quality, cost, and time.

Each has a defined use. Quantity answers the question of "How many?". How many units were produced? How many customers were not satisfied? How many projects overran their budgets? How many orders did we fill today? Quantifiable data are most preferred by organizations and, typically, most applicable for variable analysis.

Not everything, however, is precisely quantifiable. In many cases, the question is qualitative: "How good?". How satisfied were our customers with this product? To what degree are employees concerned about this procedure? How much fade was there in the color? Qualitative questions are quite often more difficult to answer. In many cases, more subjective criteria must be employed. Interviews, surveys, and focus group sessions are tools used quite often.

Of course, there are many qualitative questions that can be answered empirically as well. How long were the scratches? How deep? How many

What to Measure

Measurement Criteria

technical or word processing errors on average do we have in a technical report? Once again, the measurement tool and technique must correspond to the type of information needed.

The third category is cost. Cost per unit or per sub-unit is a good reference point for many items.

The fourth category is time. Time may be related to both throughput and output. How long does it take for a transaction to go through the process? What is the process cycle time? How long does this step take? How long will it take for this order to be fulfilled? Are we conforming to schedule? These are typical questions related to time.

Input, throughput and output data may all be appropriately measured against one or more of these criteria. None is inherently better than any other. As a set of categories, however, they help frame the thinking that will allow the best set of measurement tools, criteria and processes to be established.

Measurement is not established for the purpose of inspecting, finding fault and assigning blame. It is a critical tool for process users, owners and the management of the firm. Measurement enables the process to achieve its goals through continuous improvement, thus increasing the competitive advantage of the firm.

The Dynamics of Process Measurement

The Act of Measuring

Effective process design builds self-monitoring into the process. Input, throughput and output at critical points in the process need to be measured. These are typically hand-off points or process interfaces where the cumulative activities of adding value during the process begin, end, and begin again. Many major processes do not include specific steps that require this. This attribute can be done as a manual or computerized activity. The key is that acceptance into the next process phase is controlled. Acceptable inputs are consistently fed into the process and generate output consistent with the process objectives. This culminates in the final arbiter of process capability - the customer's satisfaction with the process output.

The ability of the reengineered process to meet the required objectives crystallized in the process vision must be measured. The reengineering model provides a check and balance in the design phase. It ensures that the new process is capable of meeting its objectives. The process capability analysis stage requires the reengineering team to test that the process outputs and inputs are assessed satisfactorily in terms of usefulness, consistency, freedom from defects, and variability. The analysis stage also ensures that the overall design is capable of meeting the demands of the vision elements.

The Dynamics of Process Measurement

When to Measure: The Pilot Implementation

The best measure of process effectiveness and efficiency should be assessed at the pilot implementation stage. At this stage, the built-in monitors and process outcomes can be clearly tested to ensure that objectives are being met.

While pilot implementation is important, the full implementation of a reengineered business process is the litmus test of its ultimate success. Often areas that worked successfully at the pilot stage fail or do not perform as required in full scale implementation. The monitoring systems in place may even fail. Although what is being measured is the same in full implementation as in the pilot, change during full implementation is much more complex and riskier. Piloting the process at an appropriate site and within a business context where the success rate is considered high is the best way to ensure that the redesigned process can be "de-bugged" before full roll out.

To avoid as many major full implementation changes as possible, there are some other options if piloting not feasible. These are forms of prototyping. Computer technology can allow an entire process to be prototyped with simulation techniques assessing the process design's viability under varying conditions. While such prototyping is limited, the measurement points can be set in place and the design principles tested.

The Dynamics of Process Measurement

An alternative manual prototype test is to repeat a technique used in the diagnosis stage of the reengineering. This is performing a paper based information test of the redesigned process. The limitation of this method is that the paper based "trail" cannot be tested against a live process.

It is recommended that pilot testing be performed as the model indicates. The costs, and organizational and business risks saved by piloting far outweigh the savings of not piloting.

Benefits of the Pilot Measures

In the pilot test phase, the reengineering teams make appropriate changes to the process design or to organizational behaviors that are required for successful implementation. Frequently, the issues confronted by reengineering teams are not design defects but organizational structures and behaviors that are ill suited or have not been developed sufficiently for the reengineered process. This illustrates the need for reengineering teams to be aware of the behavioral development required by the people involved in the process.

At the pilot test stage, it is the responsibility of the reengineering team, with steering team support, to address these issues with sensitivity and foresight. This will prevent alienation of key personnel who need to commit to the new process.

Assessing the Success of the Reengineering Effort

Expected Time Frames

The success of any major transformational change effort needs to be measured over years rather than months. This does not mean to infer that reengineering core business processes will not deliver short term successes. The fact that non-value added activities have been eliminated and output delivery is now process driven rather than functionally driven will allow the organization to reap immediate benefits. These will usually be felt as process cost reductions and more effective throughput which decreases cycle time. The short term measurable gains are usually seen as internal efficiency gains.

The impact of radically altering the way work is done to respond more effectively to customer requirements and the future state of business may take longer to materialize. Organizational structures need to adapt more effectively to the change as do people's skills and behaviors. As this occurs, the long term benefits of the reengineering effort begin to show in the measurement indices required by the process vision and its critical success factors.

Customers are slow to change their perceptions of their suppliers. Their interpretation of supplier responsiveness to their needs will change as the customer's old paradigms slowly shift. Market share will grow in direct relationship to customer acceptance of the changes realized by reengineering.

Assessing the Success of the Reengineering Effort

Measurable Business Indicators

The table below shows measurable business indicators of the reengineering effort in relation to type and positive change over the short and long term. The actual indicators will differ depending upon the type of process reengineered, the process vision and the related critical success factors.

Short Term Indicators

- Lowered process overhead cost
- Reduced product/service delivery cost
- Increased cycle time
- Reduced resource costs
- Fewer defects per unit delivered
- Less waste

Long Term Indicators

- Higher market share
- Higher product/service fee - higher perceived value
- Greater customer responsiveness
- Shorter time to market
- Fewer defects per unit delivered
- Less waste

Summary

The experience that a business unit goes through in reengineering a core business process has multiple lasting results. The impact on the organization as a whole can only be measured in the long term and will pay dividends on an ongoing basis well into the future.

One dividend is the realization that the organization has learned that re-engineering processes are not a single one time event. Process redesign must continue to meet the ever changing business environment. Once an organization has learned this lesson it has begun to master the art of continuous improvement, whose fundamental yet dramatic nature evades so many businesses.

Bibliography

Allen, David P. and Robert Nafius. *"Dreaming and Doing: Re-engineering GTE Telephone Operations."* Planning Review, Mar/Apr, 1992.

Allio, Michael K. *"Argument Against Adopting a 'Process' Mentality."* Planning Review, Jan/Feb 1993.

Barton, Richard S. *"Xerox CEO Was Organizational Architect."* Network, May, 1993.

Boar, Bernard H. *Art of Strategic Planning for Information Technology.* John Wiley & Sons, 1993.

Boston Consulting Group. *Reengineering and Beyond.* Boston Consulting Group, 1993.

Buday, Robert S. *"Reengineering One Firm's Product Development and Another's Service Delivery."* Planning Review, Mar/Apr 1992.

Byrne, John A. *"Reengineering: Beyond the Buzzword."* Business Week, 5/24/93, p12, 2p.

Carr, David K. *Break Point: Business Process Redesign.* Coopers & Lybrand, 1992.

Cherry, C. Kevin. *"Innovating Business Process Change."* Network, April, 1993.

Bibliography

Cole, Christopher, Michael L. Clark, and Carl Nemec. *"Reengineering Information Systems at Cincinnati Milacron."* Planning Review, May/June, 1993.

Conner, Daryl. *Managing at the Speed of Change.* Villand Books, 1993.

Davenport, Thomas H. *"Need Radical Innovation and Continuous Improvement? Integrate Process Reengineering and TQM."* Planning Review, May/June, 1993.

Davenport, Thomas H. *Process Innovation: Reengineering Work Through Information Technology.* Harvard Business School Press, 1993.

Davis, Tim. *"Reengineering in Action."* Planning Review, July/Aug, 1993.

Drucker, Peter F. *Managing the Future.* Truman Tally Books, 1992.

Duck, J.D. *"Managing Change: The Art of Balancing."* Harvard Business Review, Nov/Dec, 1993.

Ettorre, Barbara and Catherine Romano. *"Human Resources: Requirement for Reengineering."* Management Review, June 1994.

Fagiano, David. *"Reengineering Swiss Cheese."* Management Review, June, 1994.

Bibliography

Furey, Timothy. *"Applying Information Technology to Reengineering."* Planning Review, Nov/Dec, 1993.

Furey, Timothy. *"A Six Step Guide to Process Reengineering."* Planning Review, Mar/Apr, 1992.

Gendron, George. *"A Do-It-Yourself Classic."* Inc. Magazine, June 93, p14.

Guterl, Fred and Jonathan B. Levine. *"On the Continent, a New Era is Also Dawning."* Business Week, 6/14/93, p61, 1p.

Hall, G., Rosenthal, J. and J. Wade. *"How to Make Reengineering Really Work."* Harvard Business Review, Nov/Dec 93, p119, 13p.

Hammer, M. *"Reengineering Work: Don't Automate, Obliterate."* Harvard Business Review, Jul/Aug 90, p104, 9p.

Hammer, Michael and James Champy. *"The Promise of Reengineering."* Fortune, 5/3/93, p94, 4p.

Hammer, Michael and James Champy. *Re-engineering the Corporation.* Harper Collins, 1993.

Handy, Charles B. *Age of Unreason.* Harvard Business School Press, 1990.

Bibliography

Harrison, D. Brian and Maurice D. Pratt. "*A Methodology for Reengineering Business Processes.*" Planning Review, Mar/Apr, 1993.

Housel, Thomas, Arthur Bell, and Valery Kanevsky. "*Calculating the Value of Reengineering at Pacific Bell.*" Planning Review, Jan/Feb, 1994.

Housel, Thomas J., Chris J. Morris, and Christopher Westland. "*Business Process Reengineering at Pacific Bell.*" Planning Review, May/June, 1993.

Johansson, Henry J. *Business Process Re-engineering: Breakpoint Strategies for Market Dominance.* John Wiley & Sons, 1993.

Katzenbach, Jon R. and Douglas K. Smith. "*Rules for Managing Cross-functional Reengineering Teams.*" Planning Review, Mar/Apr, 1992.

Kirby, Philip (AMA Membership Department). "*The New CEO: The Engine of Reengineering.*" Management Review, June 1994.

Manganelli, Raymond L. and Mark M. Klein. "*Reengineering: Mistakes and Pitfalls.*" Network, November 1993.

Manganelli, Raymond L. and Mark M. Klein. "*A Framework for Reengineering.*" Management Review, June 1994.

Bibliography

Mattimore, Bryan W. *99% Inspiration: Tips, Tales & Techniques for Liberating Your Business Creativity.* AMACOM, 1994.

McWilliams, Gary. *"Putting a Shine on Shoe Operations."* Business Week, 6/14/93, p59, 1/2p.

Morris, Daniel. *Reengineering Your Business.* McGraw-Hill, 1993.

Norman, David. *"Changing the Focus of Strategy."* Network, April 1993.

Randall, Robert. *"The Reengineer."* Planning Review, May/June, 1993.

Resnick, Harold S. *"The Challenge of Organizational Transformation."* Work Systems Informational Series, Volume 1, July 1993.

Resnick, Harold S. *"Reengineering the Organization."* Work Systems Informational Series, Volume 3, March 1994.

Resnick, Harold S. and Sandy H. Brown. *People Productivity: A Validated Model for Measurement.* Work Systems Products, Inc. 1989.

Resnick, Harold S. and Don D. DeWolfe. *Total Quality Core Program.* Volumes 1-6. Work Systems Associates, Inc., 1993.

Richman, Theodor and Charles Koontz. *"How Benchmarking Can Improve Business Reengineering."* Planning Review, Nov/Dec, 1993.

Bibliography

Rigby, Darrell. *"The Secret History of Process Reengineering."* Planning Review, Mar/Apr 1992.

Rothschild, William. *"Caretakers Can't Reengineer."* Network, October 1993.

Stewart, Thomas A. and Joyce E. Davis. *"Reengineering: The Hot New Management Tool."* Fortune, 8/23/93, p40, 6p.

Stow, Ralph P. *"Reengineering by Objectives."* Planning Review, May/June, 1993.

Therrien, Lois. *"Consultant, Reengineer Thyself."* Business Week, 4/12/93, p86, 2p.

Treece, James B. *"Improving the Soul of an Old Machine."* Business Week, 10/25/93, p134, 2p.